FOR ORGANS, PIANOS & ELECTRONIC KEYBOARDS

E-Z PLAY® TODAY

193

BRUNO M

ISBN 978-1-4803-6063-1

HAL•LEONARD®
CORPORATION

7777 W. BLUEMOUND RD. P.O. BOX 13819 MILWAUKEE, WI 53213

In Australia Contact:
Hal Leonard Australia Pty. Ltd.
4 Lentara Court
Cheltenham, Victoria, 3192 Australia
Email: ausadmin@halleonard.com.au

Visit Hal Leonard Online at
www.halleonard.com

Count on Me

Registration 4
Rhythm: Folk or Pop

Words and Music by Bruno Mars,
Ari Levine and Philip Lawrence

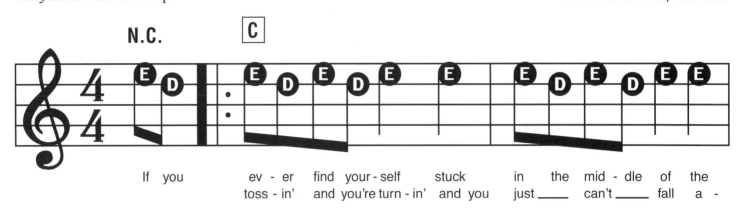

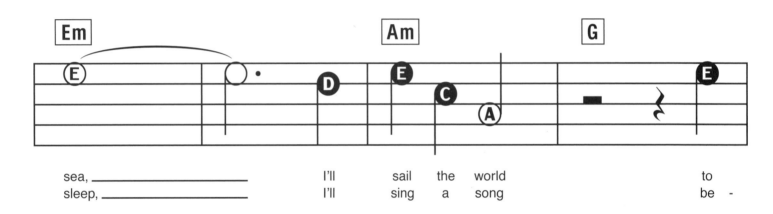

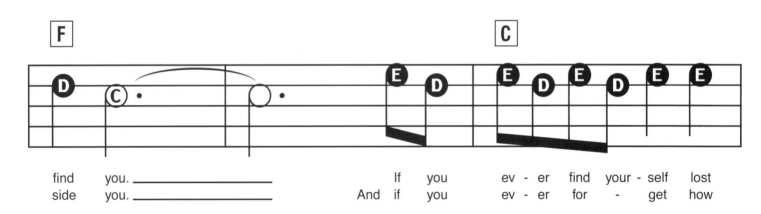

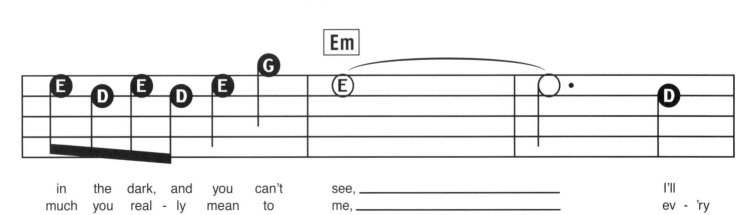

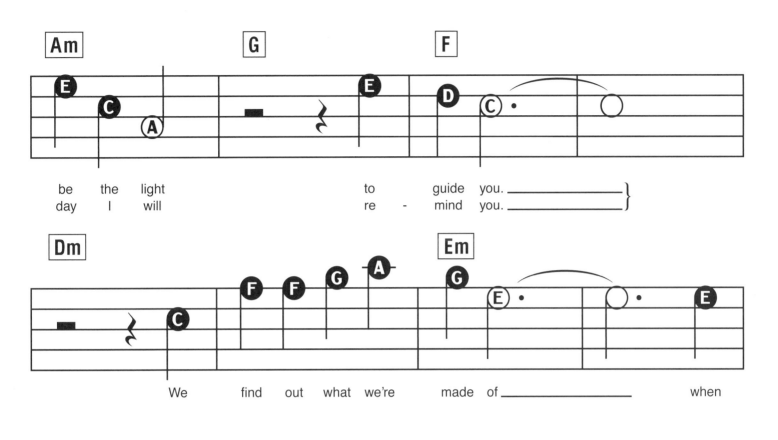

be the light   to   guide   you. _____ }
day   I   will   re -   mind   you. _____ }

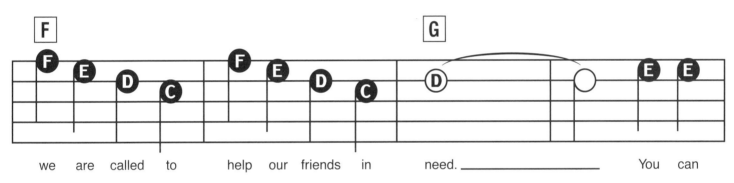

We   find   out   what   we're   made   of _____   when

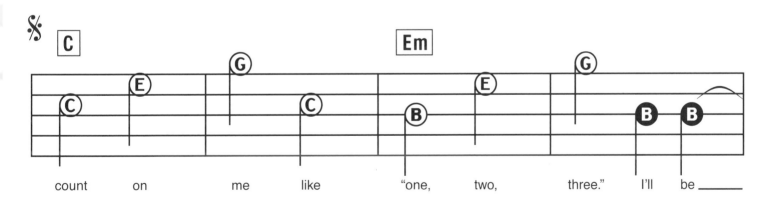

we   are   called to   help   our   friends in   need. _____   You   can

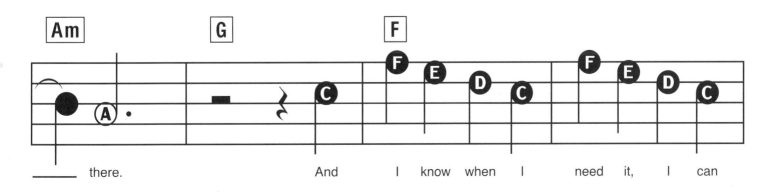

count   on   me   like   "one,   two,   three." I'll   be _____

_____ there.   And   I   know   when   I   need   it,   I   can

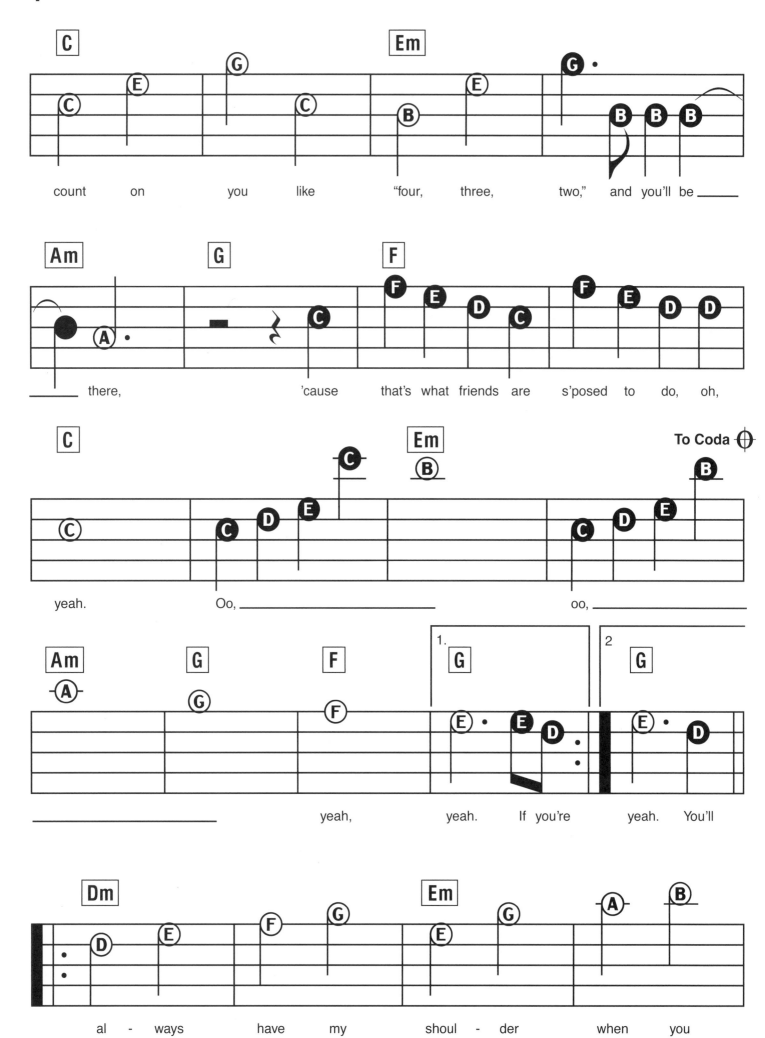

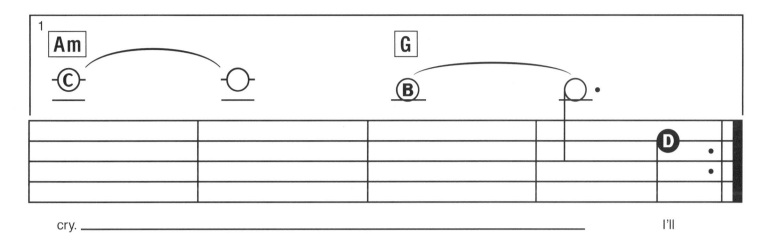

cry. _____ I'll

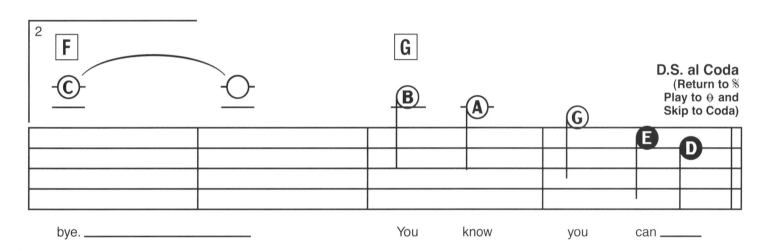

D.S. al Coda
(Return to %
Play to ⊕ and
Skip to Coda)

bye. _____ You know you can _____

CODA

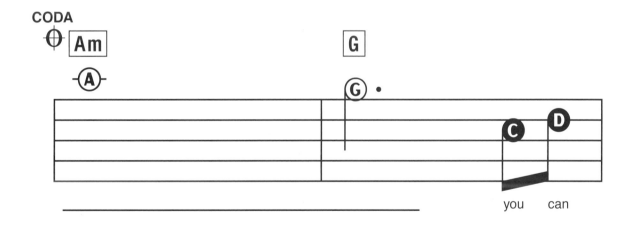

you can

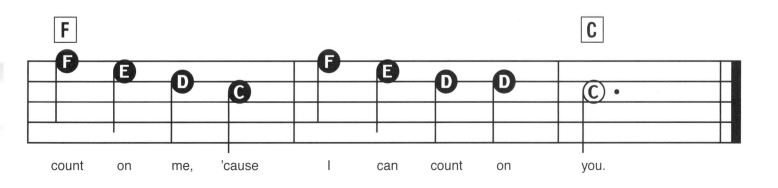

count on me, 'cause I can count on you.

Grenade

Registration 8
Rhythm: Rock or Dance

Words and Music by Bruno Mars,
Ari Levine, Philip Lawrence, Brody Brown,
Claude Kelly and Andrew Wyatt

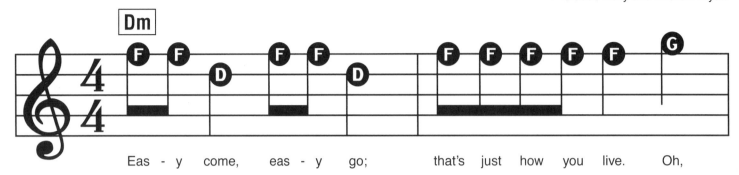

Eas - y come, eas - y go; that's just how you live. Oh,

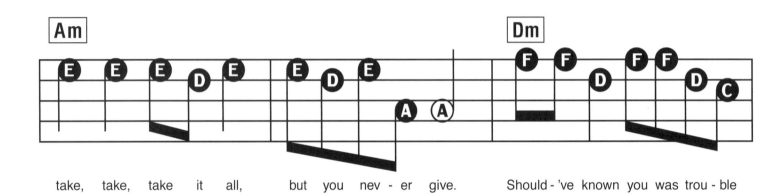

take, take, take it all, but you nev - er give. Should - 've known you was trou - ble

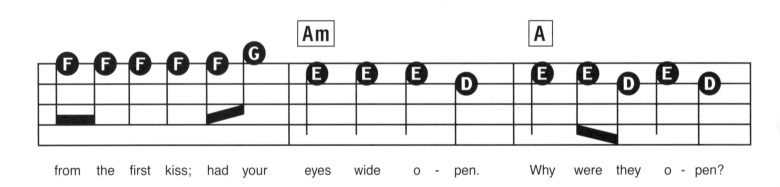

from the first kiss; had your eyes wide o - pen. Why were they o - pen?

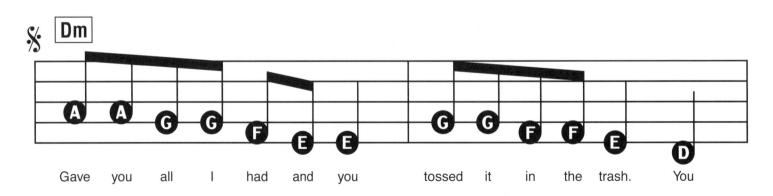

Gave you all I had and you tossed it in the trash. You

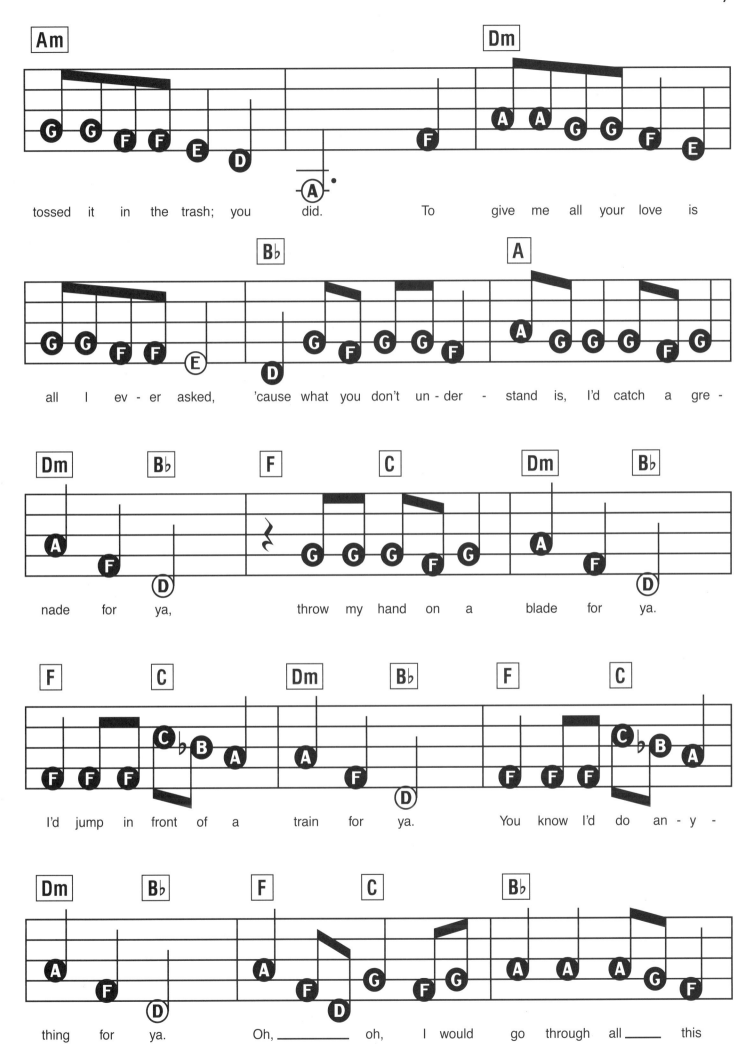

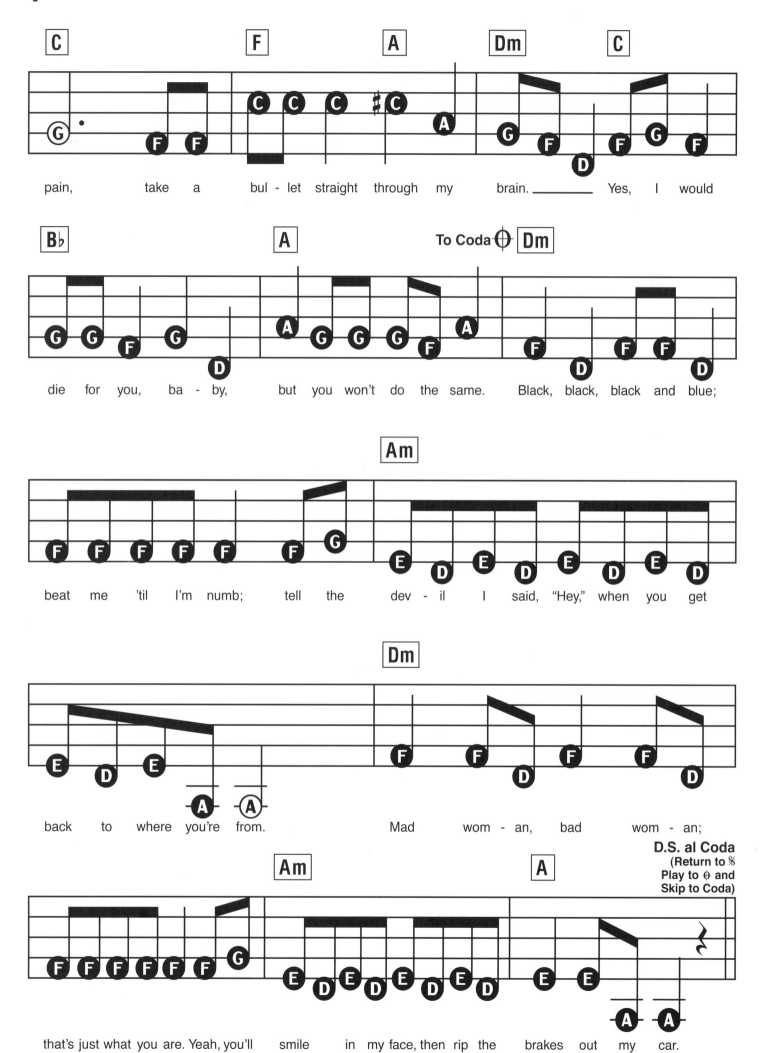

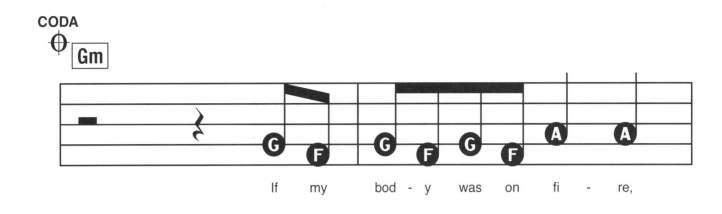

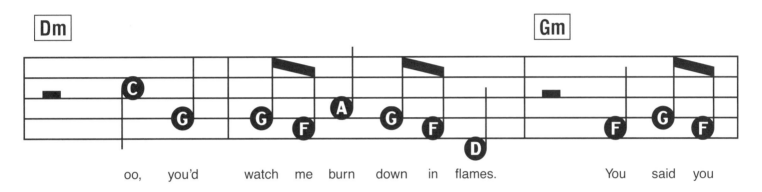

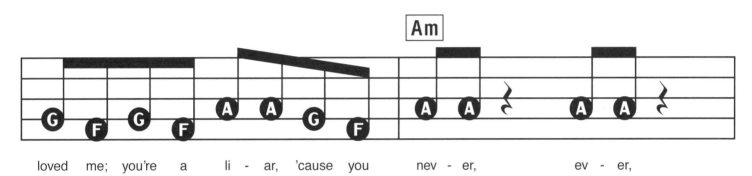

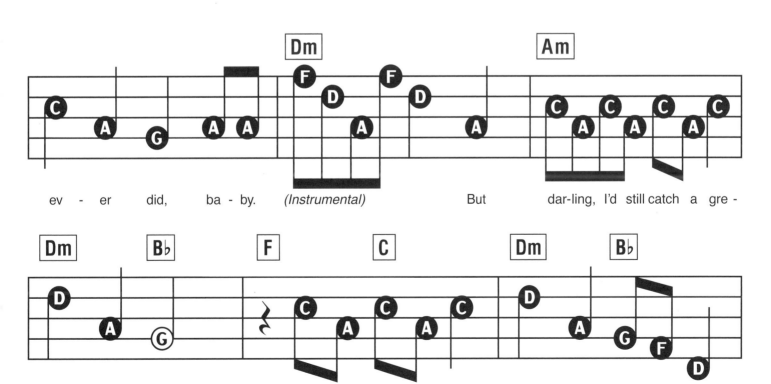

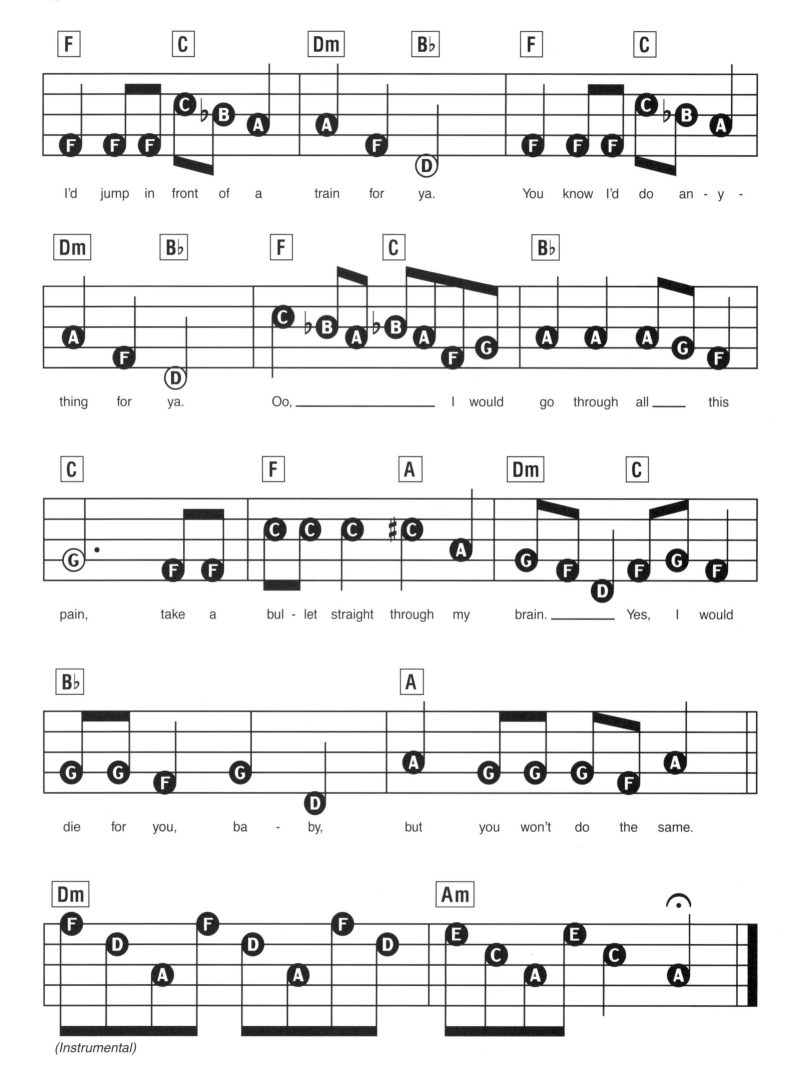

(Instrumental)

It Will Rain

from the Summit Entertainment film THE TWILIGHT SAGA: BREAKING DAWN – PART 1

Registration 8
Rhythm: 8-Beat or Rock

Words and Music by Bruno Mars,
Philip Lawrence and Ari Levine

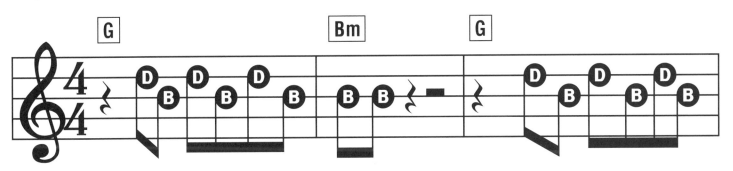

If you ev - er leave me, ba - by, leave some mor - phine at my
There's no re - li - gion that could save me, no mat - ter how long my knees are on the

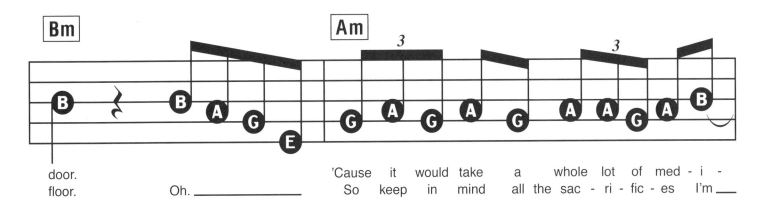

door. 'Cause it would take a whole lot of med - i -
floor. Oh. So keep in mind all the sac - ri - fic - es I'm

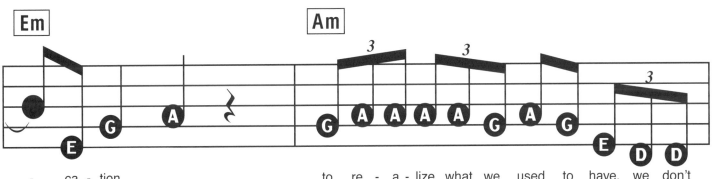

- ca - tion to re - a - lize what we used to have, we don't
mak - in' to keep you by my side and keep you from

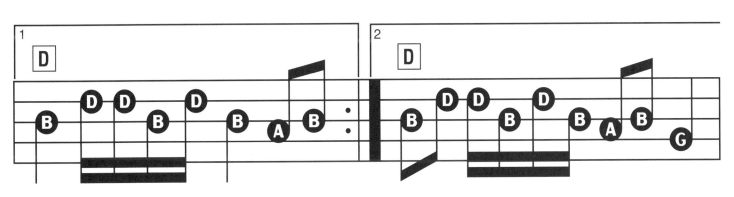

have it an - y - more. walk - in' out the door. 'Cause

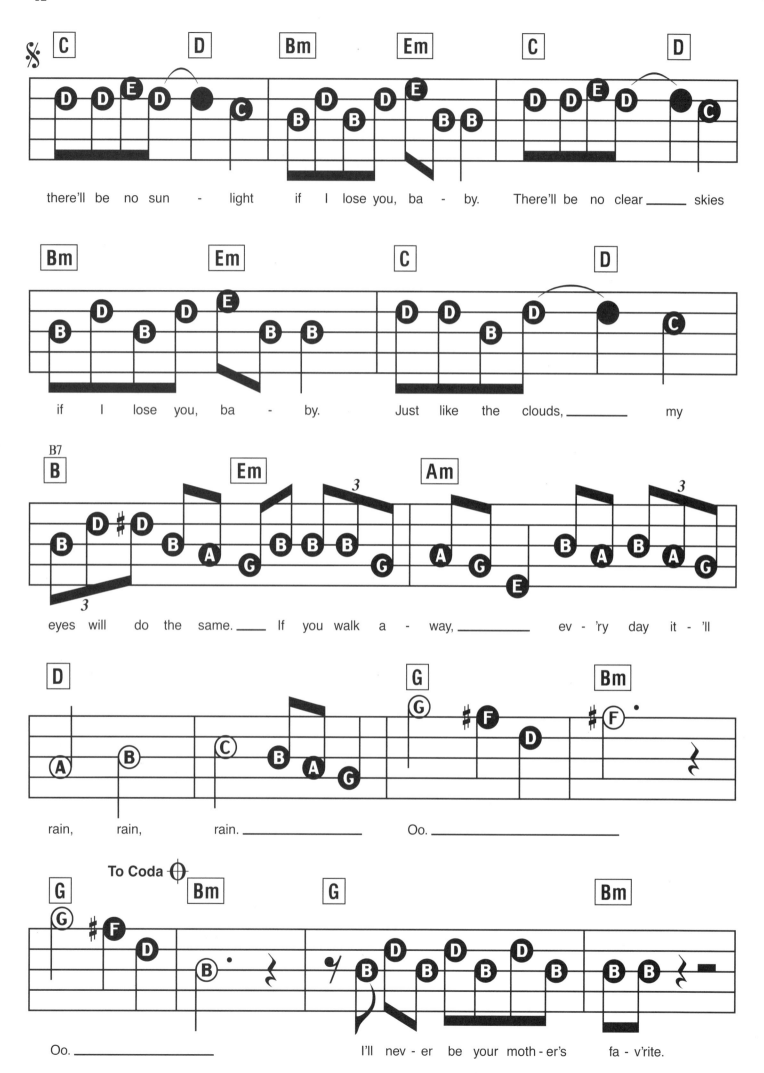

12

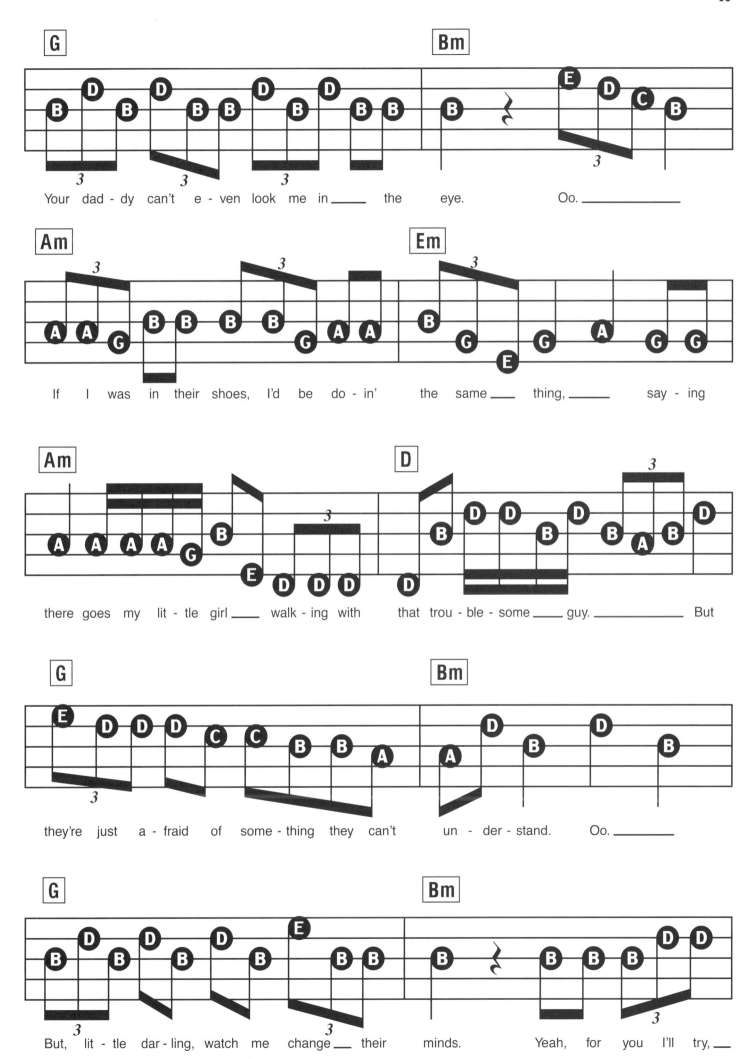

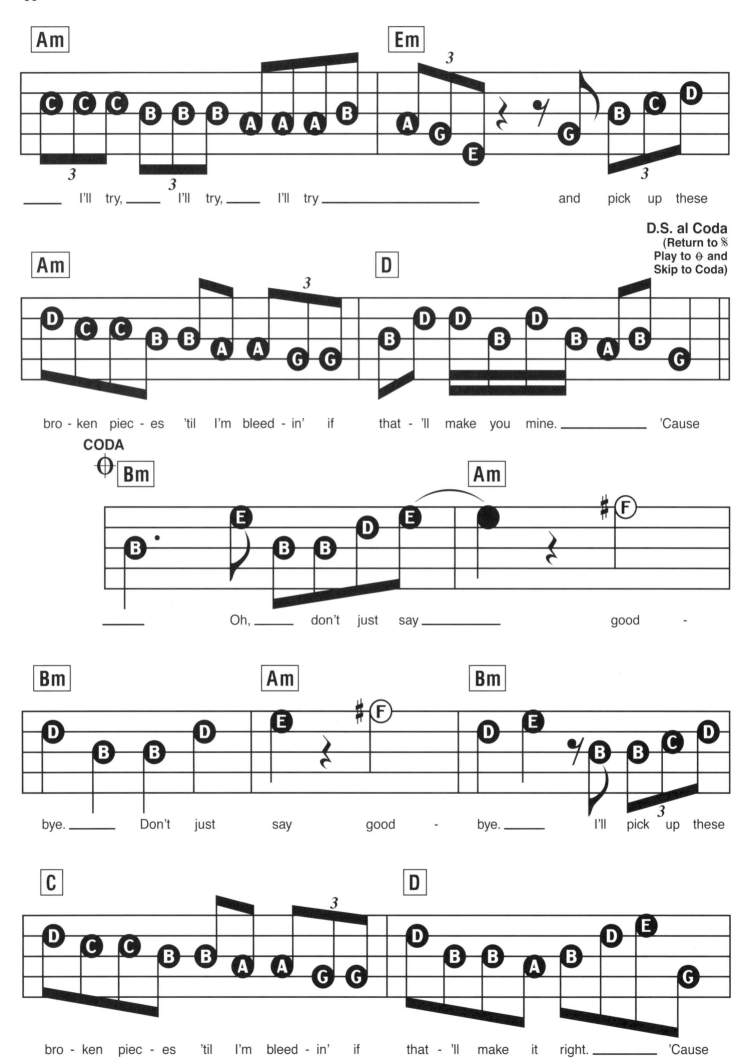

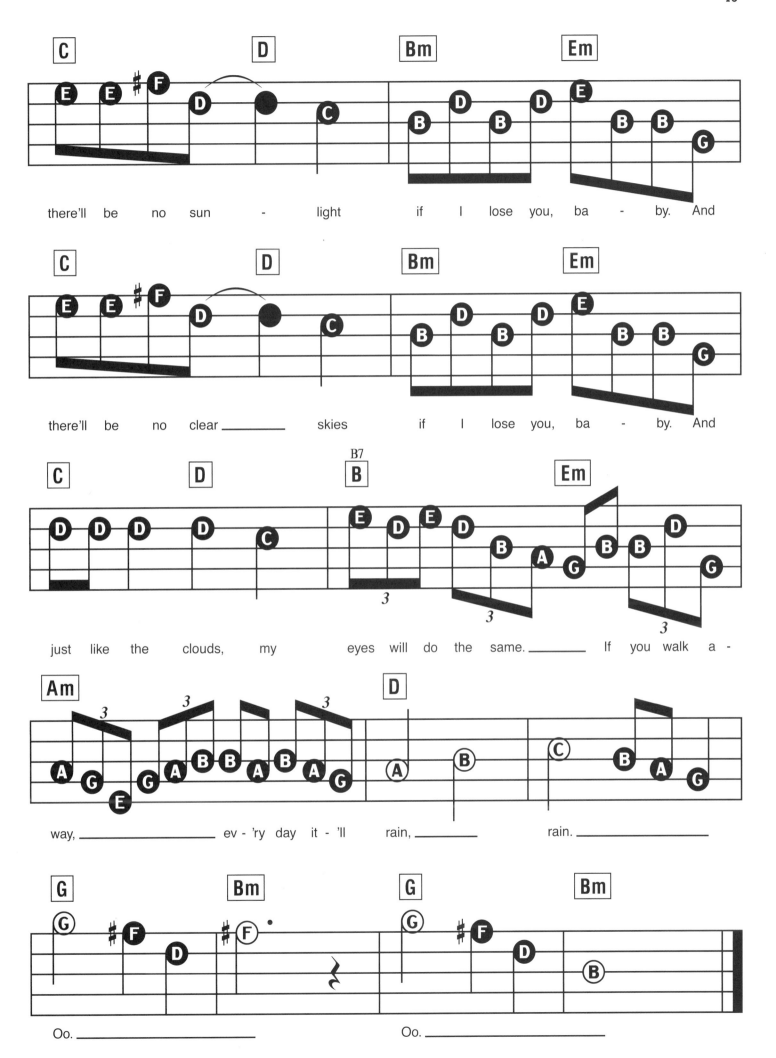

Just the Way You Are

Registration 4
Rhythm: 16-Beat or Rock

Words and Music by Bruno Mars,
Ari Levine, Philip Lawrence,
Khari Cain and Khalil Walton

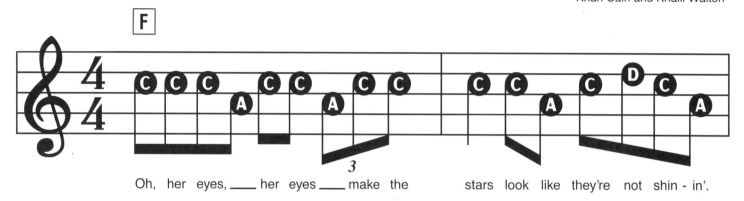

Oh, her eyes, ___ her eyes ___ make the stars look like they're not shin - in'.

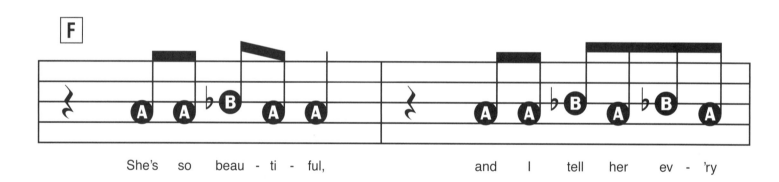

Her hair, ___ her hair ___ falls per - fect - ly with - out her try - in'.

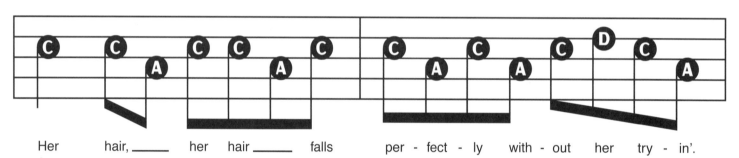

She's so beau - ti - ful, and I tell her ev - 'ry

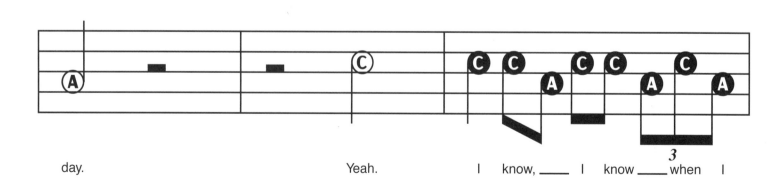

day. Yeah. I know, ___ I know ___ when I

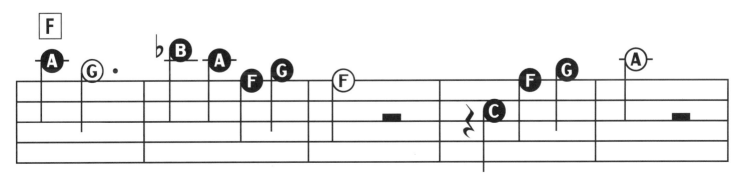

Dm

com - pli - ment her, she won't be - lieve _____ me. And it's so, _____ it's so _____ sad to

F

think that she don't see what I _____ see. But ev - 'ry time she asks me,

"Do I look o - kay?" I _____ say: When I see your

Dm

face, there's not a thing that I would change, 'cause you're a -

F

maz - ing just the way you are. And when you smile,

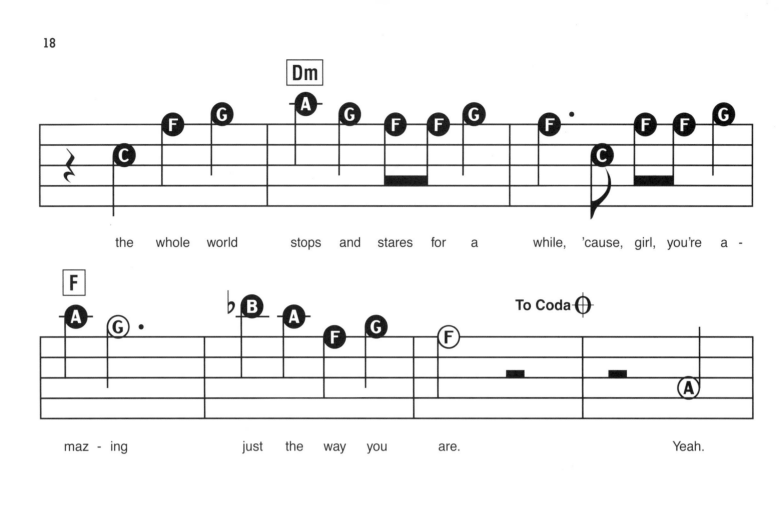

the whole world stops and stares for a while, 'cause, girl, you're a -

maz - ing just the way you are. Yeah.

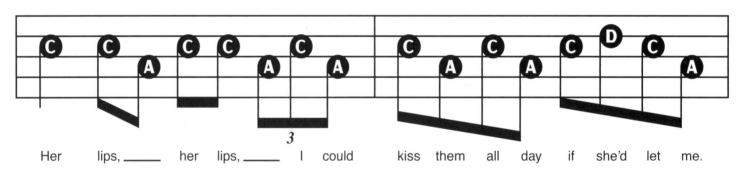

Her lips, _____ her lips, _____ I could kiss them all day if she'd let me.

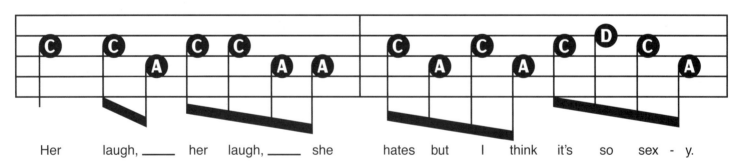

Her laugh, _____ her laugh, _____ she hates but I think it's so sex - y.

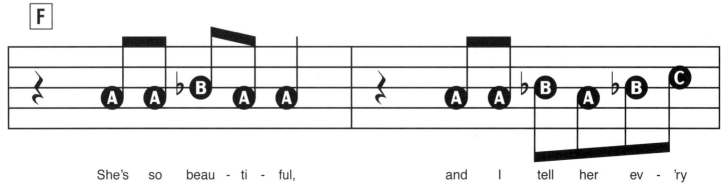

She's so beau - ti - ful, and I tell her ev - 'ry

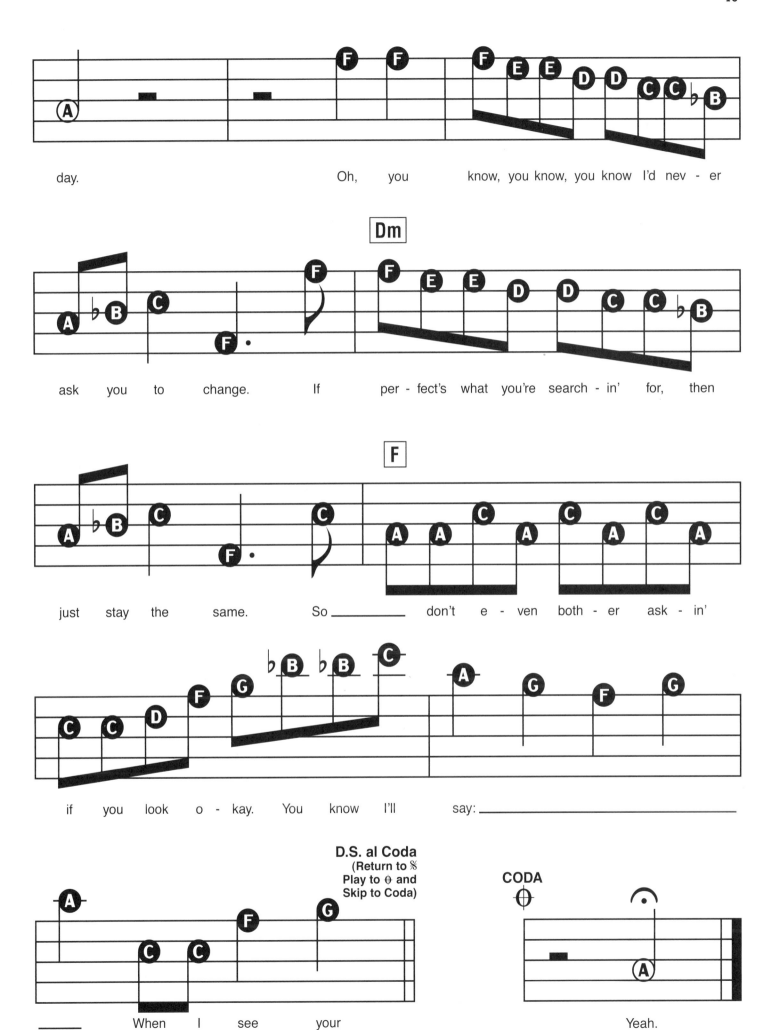

The Lazy Song

Registration 4
Rhythm: Reggae or Calypso

Words and Music by Bruno Mars,
Ari Levine, Philip Lawrence
and Keinan Warsame

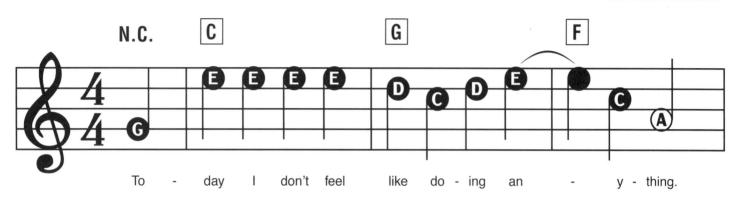

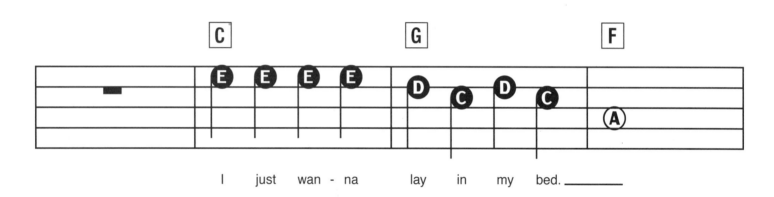

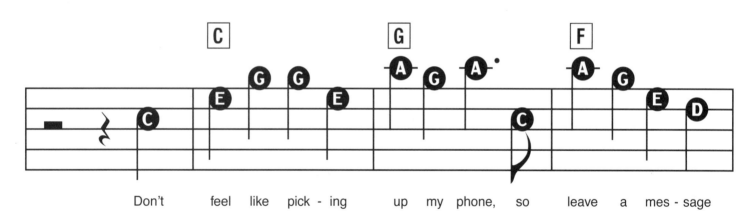

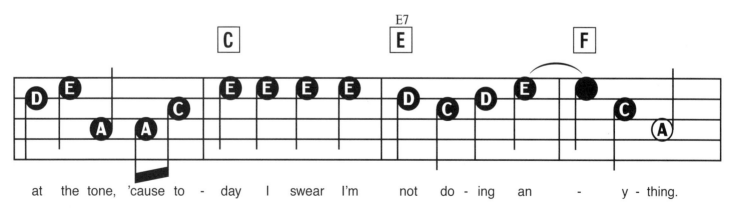

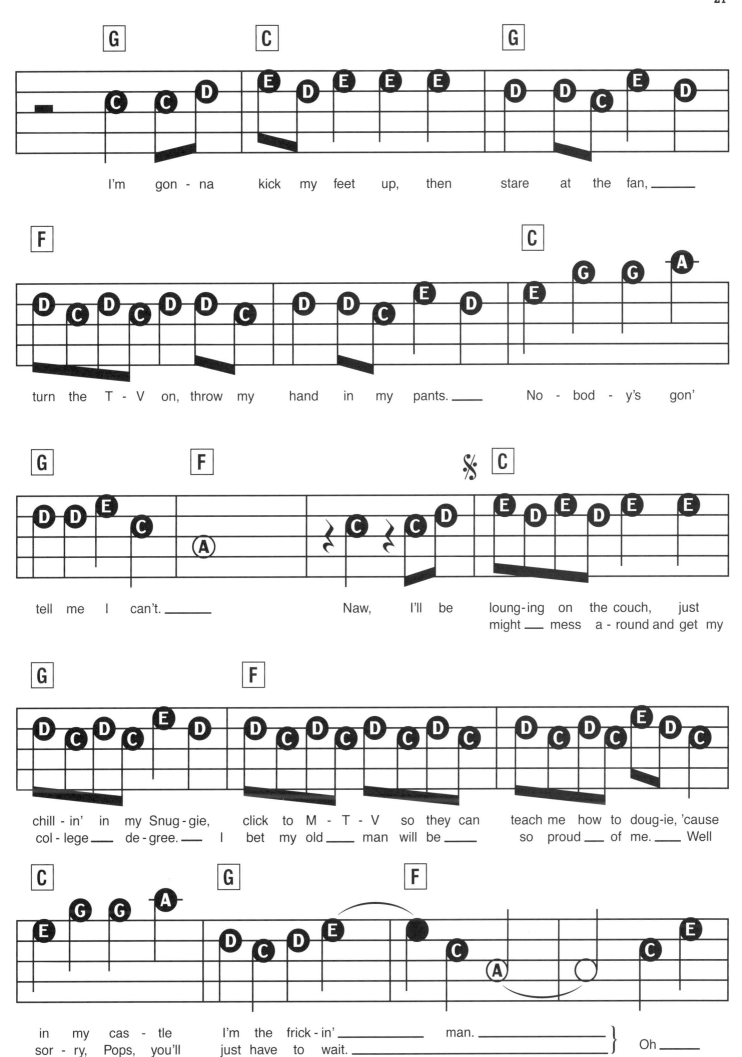

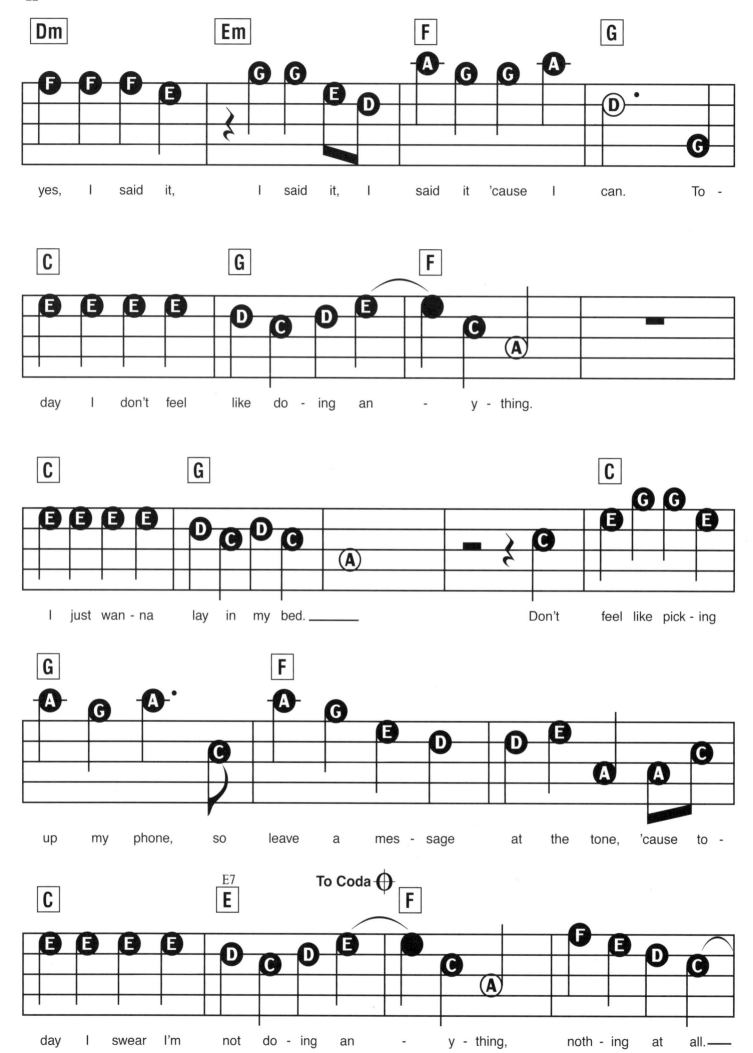

22

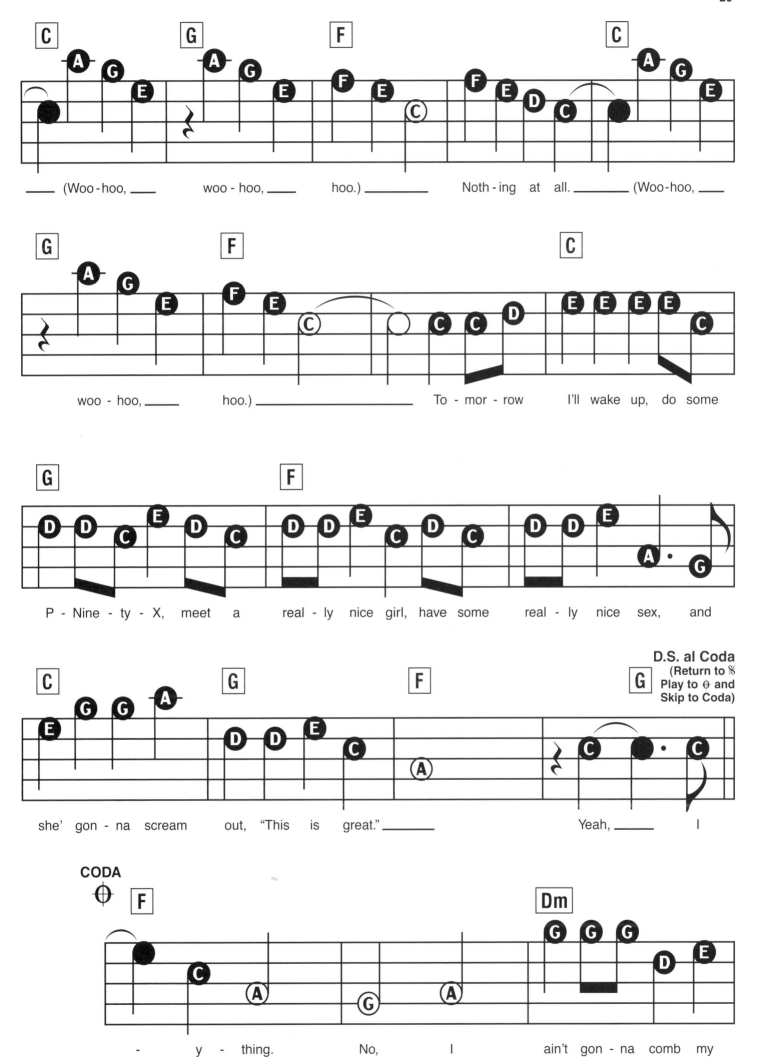

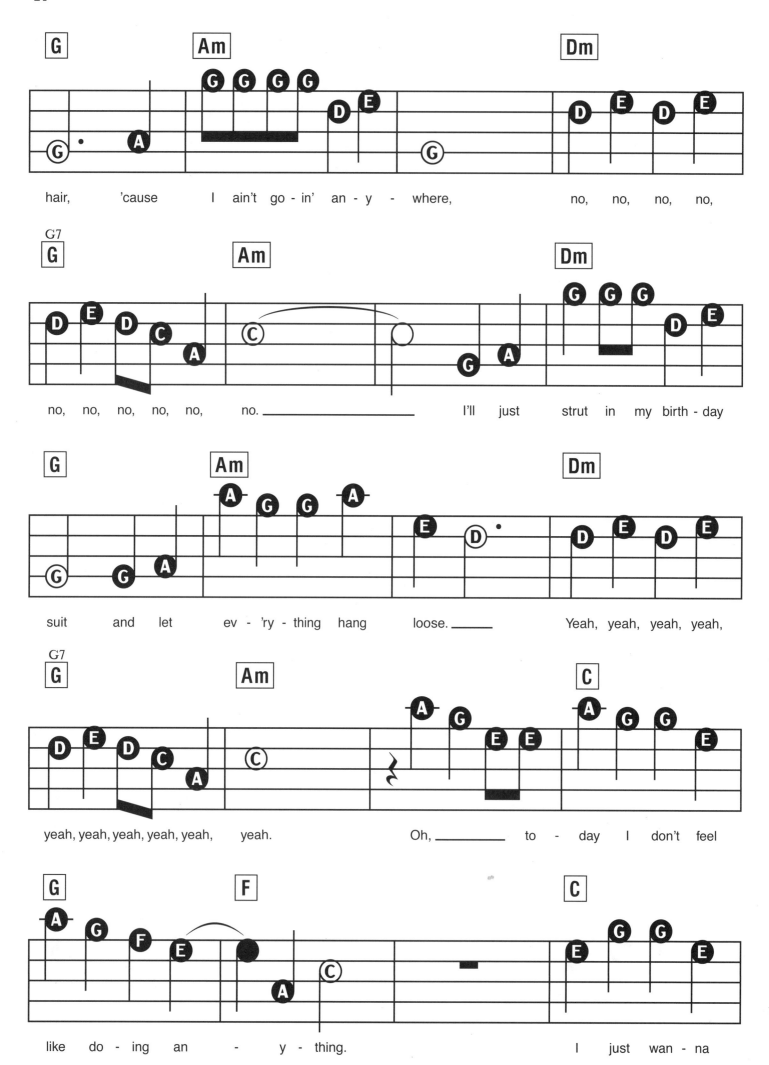

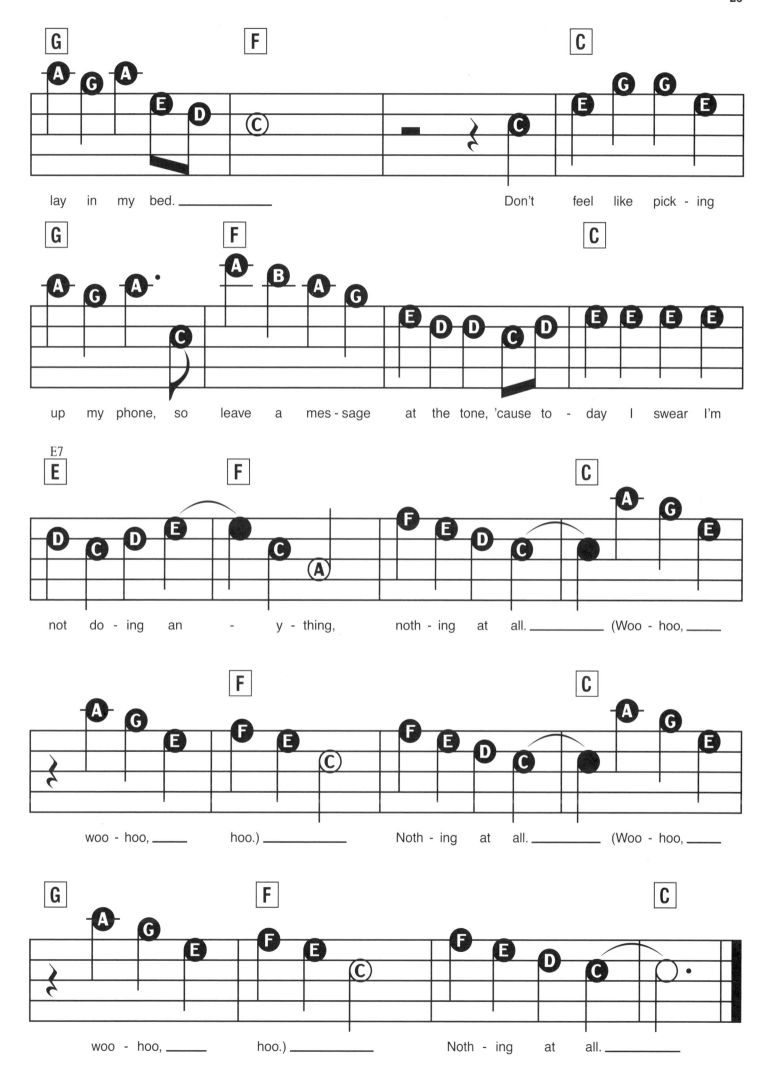

Locked Out of Heaven

Registration 8
Rhythm: Rock or Pop

Words and Music by Bruno Mars,
Ari Levine and Philip Lawrence

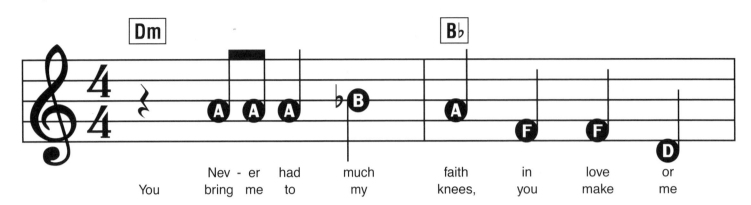

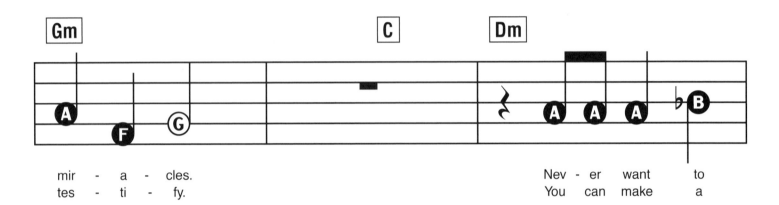

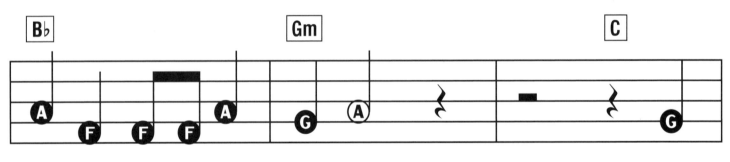

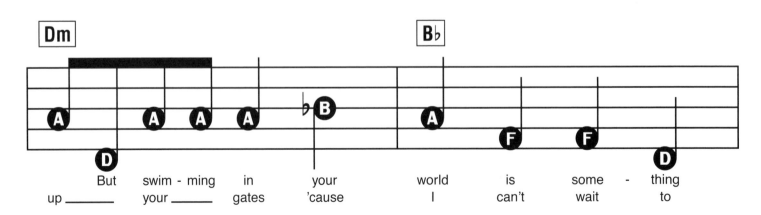

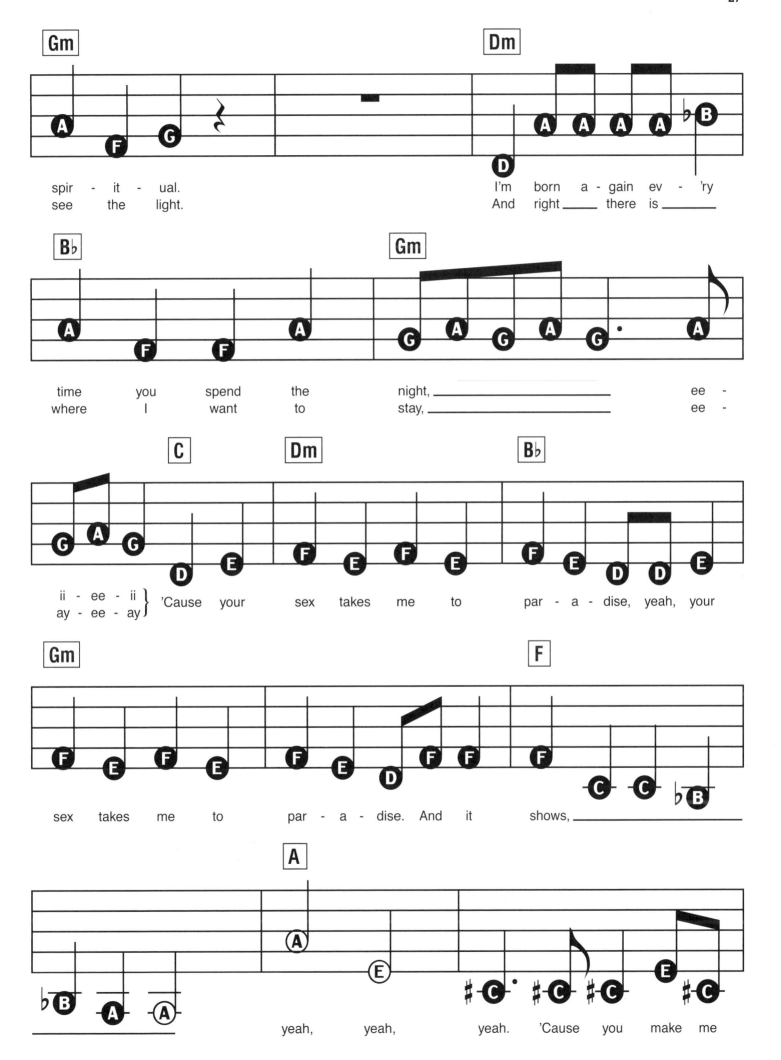

28

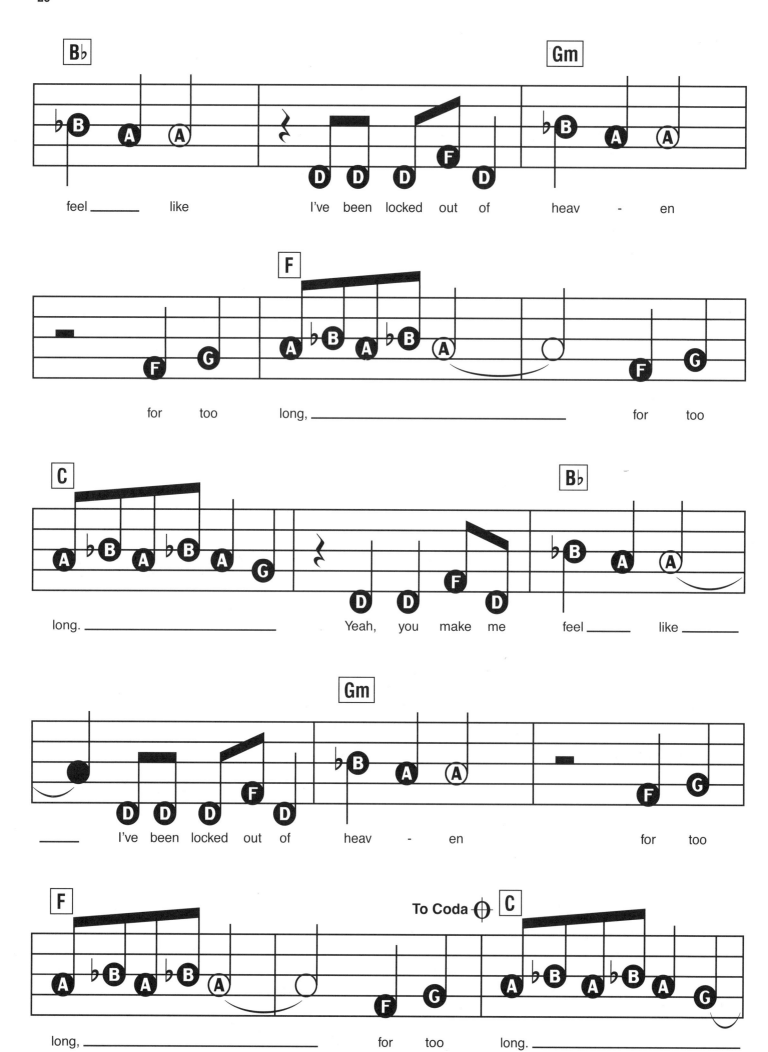

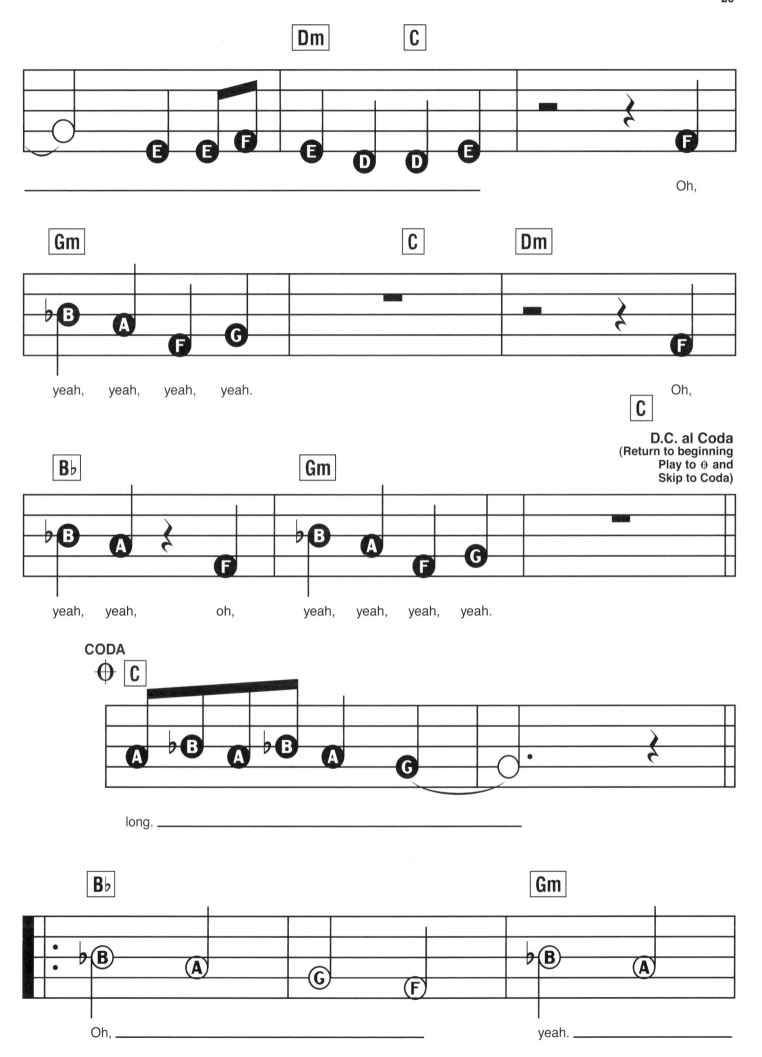

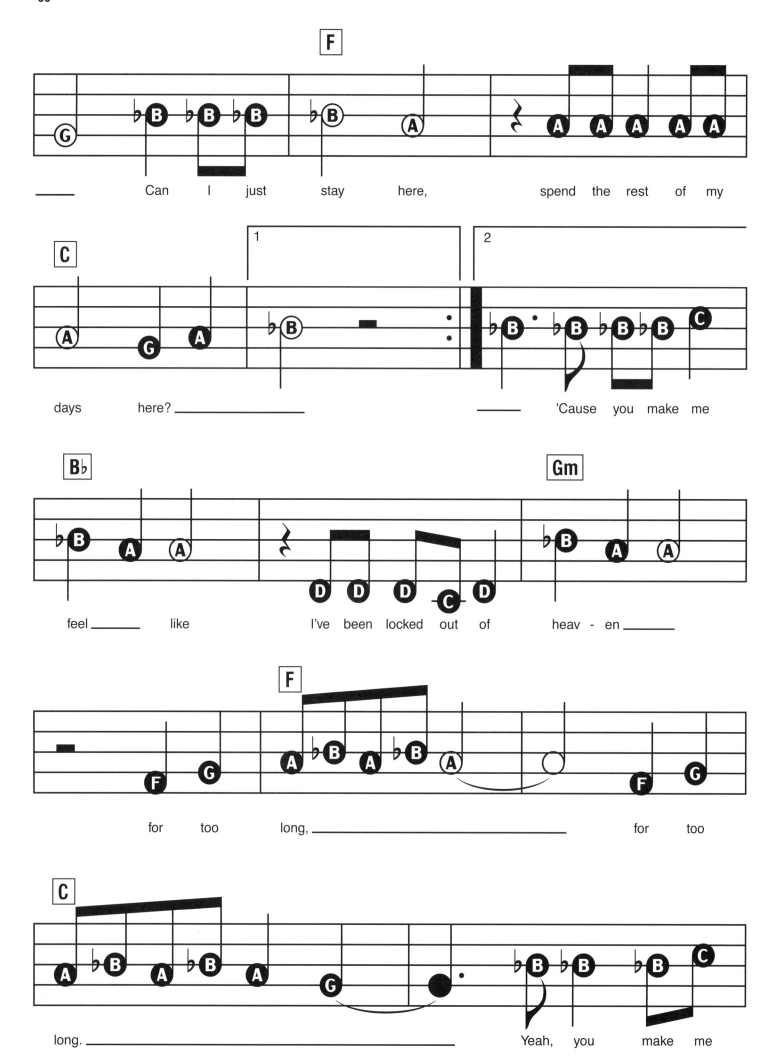

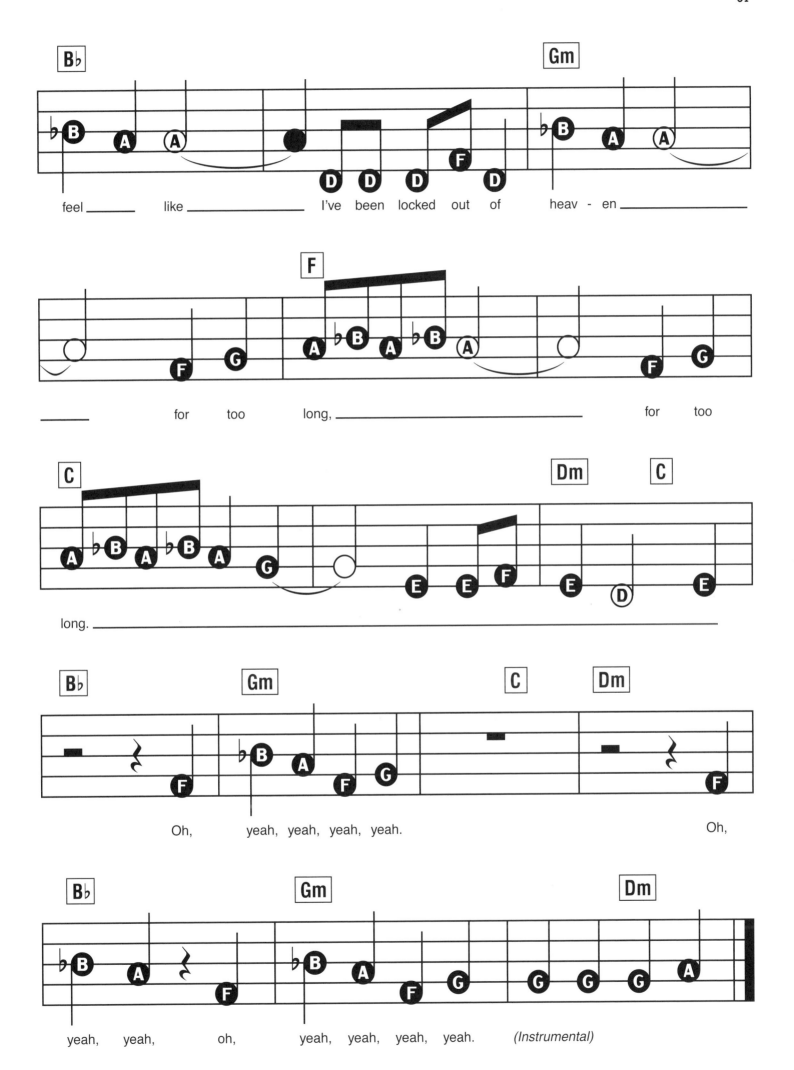

Talking to the Moon

Registration 8
Rhythm: 4/4 Ballad

Words and Music by Bruno Mars,
Ari Levine, Philip Lawrence,
Jeff Bhasker and Albert Winkler

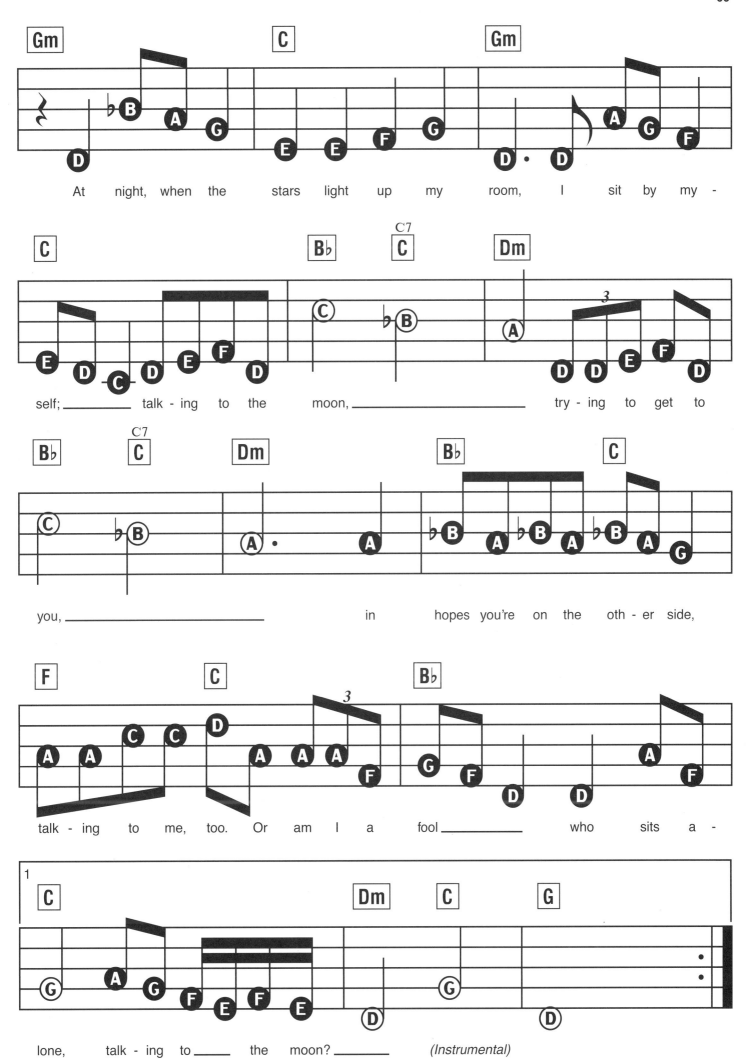

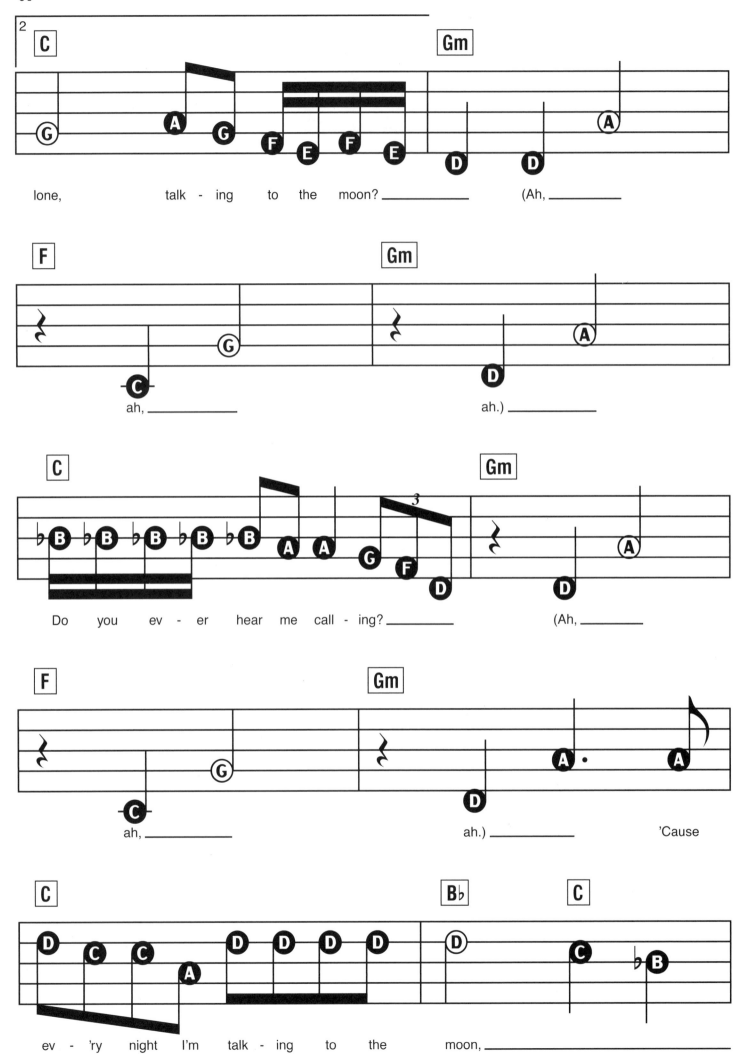

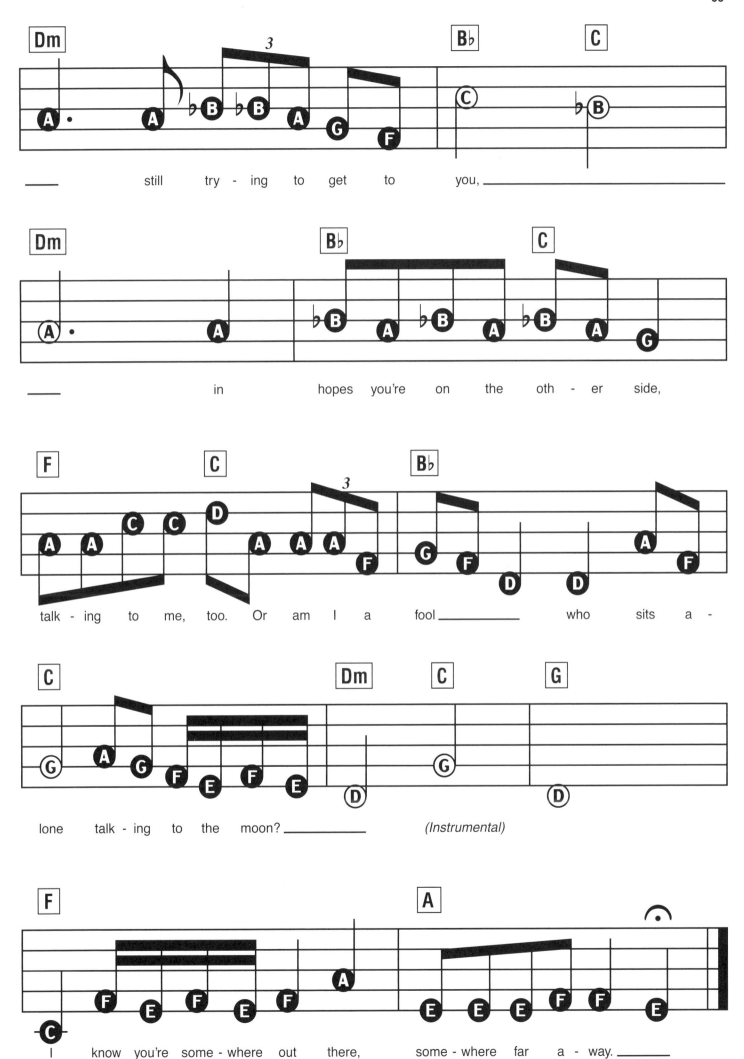

Treasure

Registration 4
Rhythm: Rock or Dance

Words and Music by Bruno Mars,
Ari Levine, Philip Lawrence
and Phredley Brown

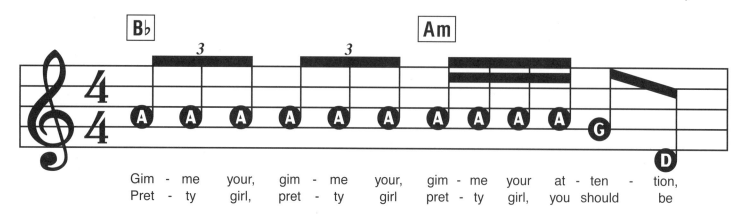

Gim - me your, gim - me your, gim - me your at - ten - tion,
Pret - ty girl, pret - ty girl pret - ty girl, you should be

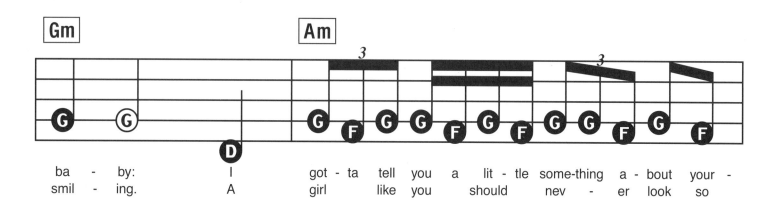

ba - by: I got - ta tell you a lit - tle some-thing a - bout your -
smil - ing. A girl like you should nev - er look so

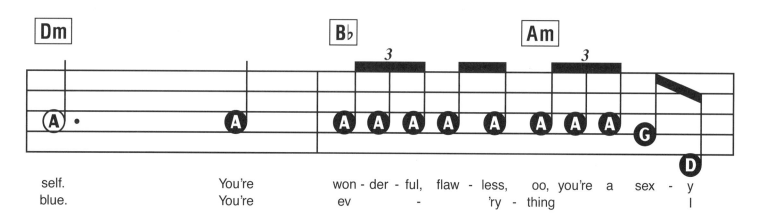

self. You're won - der - ful, flaw - less, oo, you're a sex - y
blue. You're ev - 'ry - thing I

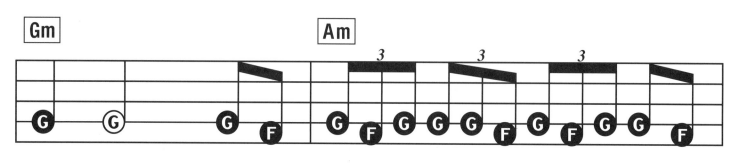

la - dy, but you walk a - round here like you wan - na be some - one
see in my dreams. I would - n't say that to you if it was - n't

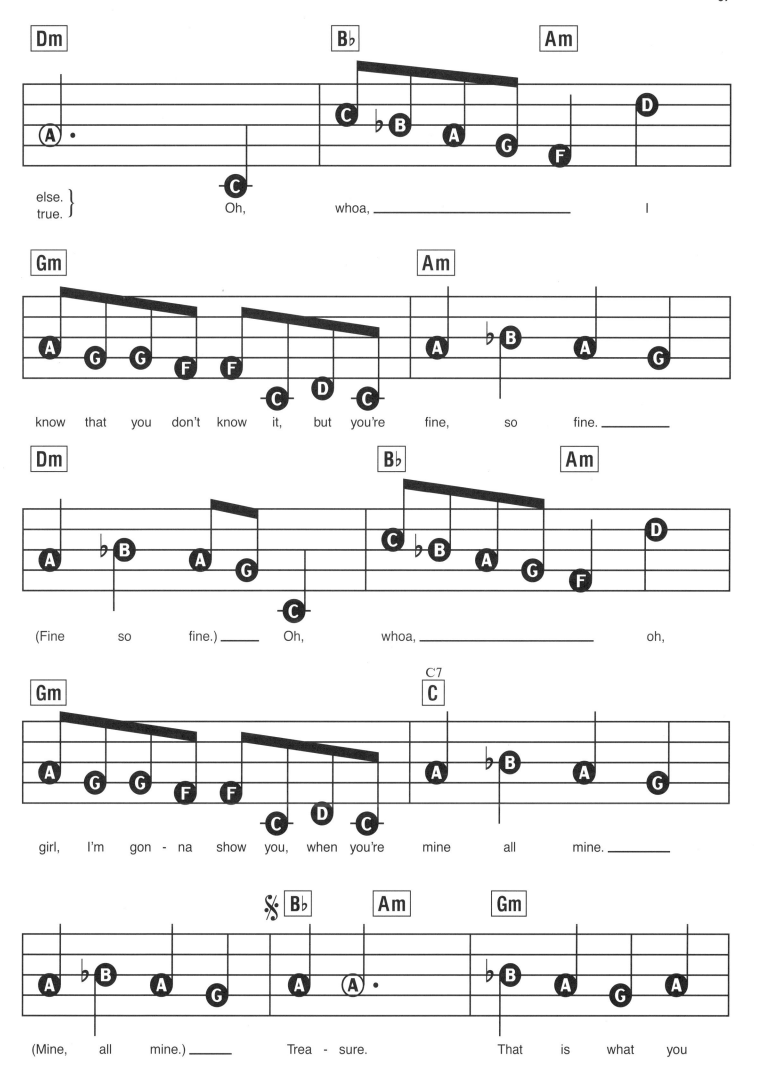

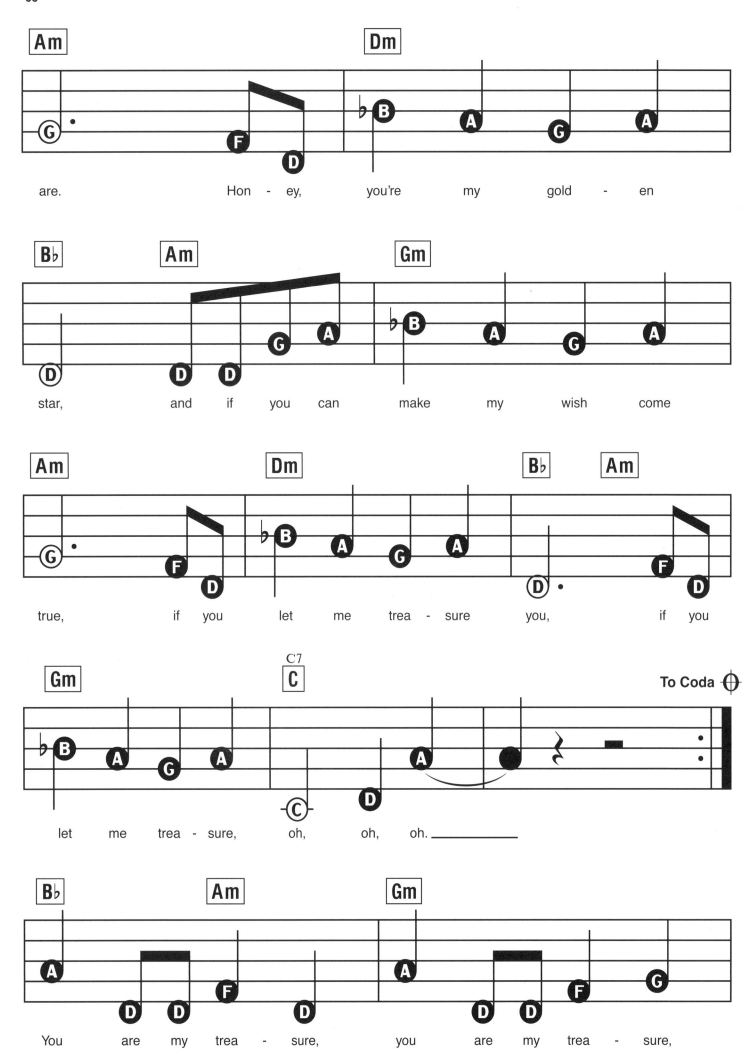

Am ... **Dm**

are. Hon - ey, you're my gold - en

B♭ **Am** **Gm**

star, and if you can make my wish come

Am **Dm** **B♭** **Am**

true, if you let me trea - sure you, if you

Gm C7 **C** To Coda ⊕

let me trea - sure, oh, oh, oh. ___

B♭ **Am** **Gm**

You are my trea - sure, you are my trea - sure,

Am

A D D F D F

you are my trea - sure yeah,

Dm

A G F A A

you, you, you, you are.

Bb

A D D F D

You are my trea - sure,

Am

Gm

A D D F G

you are my trea - sure

C7
C

A D D F D F

you are my trea - sure, yeah,

D.S. al Coda
(Return to %
Play to ⊕ and
Skip to Coda)

A G F A A

you, you, you, you are.

CODA
⊕

Bb **Am** **Gm** **1** **Am**

A G F A G G

(Instrumental)

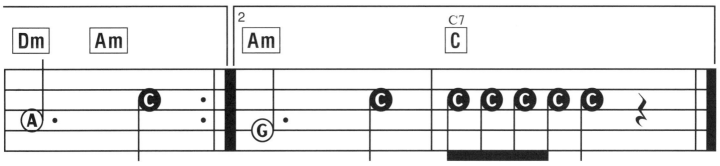

Dm **Am** **2** **Am** **C7** **C**

A C G C C C C C C

When I Was Your Man

Registration 8
Rhythm: 4/4 Ballad

Words and Music by Bruno Mars,
Ari Levine, Philip Lawrence
and Andrew Wyatt

Am   **C**   **Dm**

E E E D E E D E D C   E F F·

Same bed, but it feels just a lit - tle bit big - ger now.
My pride, my ___ e - go, my needs and my self - ish ways

G   **C**   **Em**

D D D C D D C D D C A   D E E

Our song on the ra - di - o, but it don't sound the same.
caused a good strong ___ wom - an like you to walk out my life.

Am   **C**   **Dm**

C E E E D E D E D E D C   E F G F E D

When our friends talk a - bout you, all it does is just tear me down, ___
Now I ___ nev - er get to clean up the mess I've made, ___

G   **C**

G D D D C D C D C ♭E   D D C C C D G A

'cause my heart breaks a - lit - tle when I hear ___ your name. } It all just sounds like,
and it haunts me ___ ev - 'ry time I close ___ my eyes.

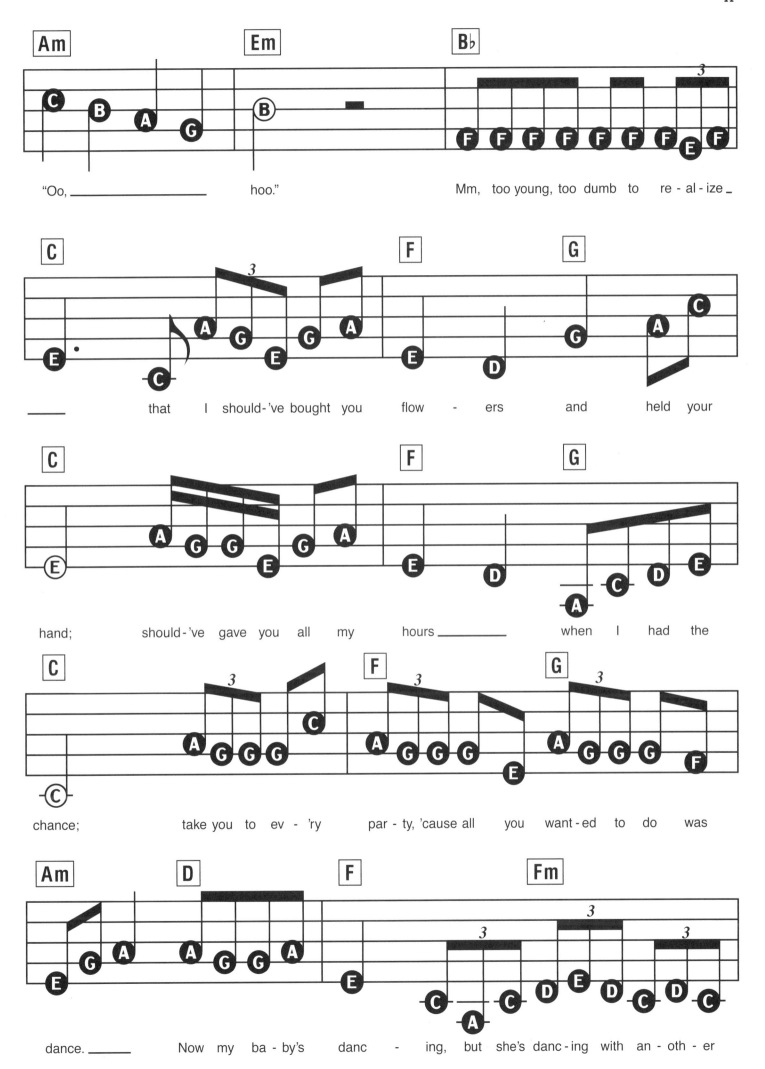

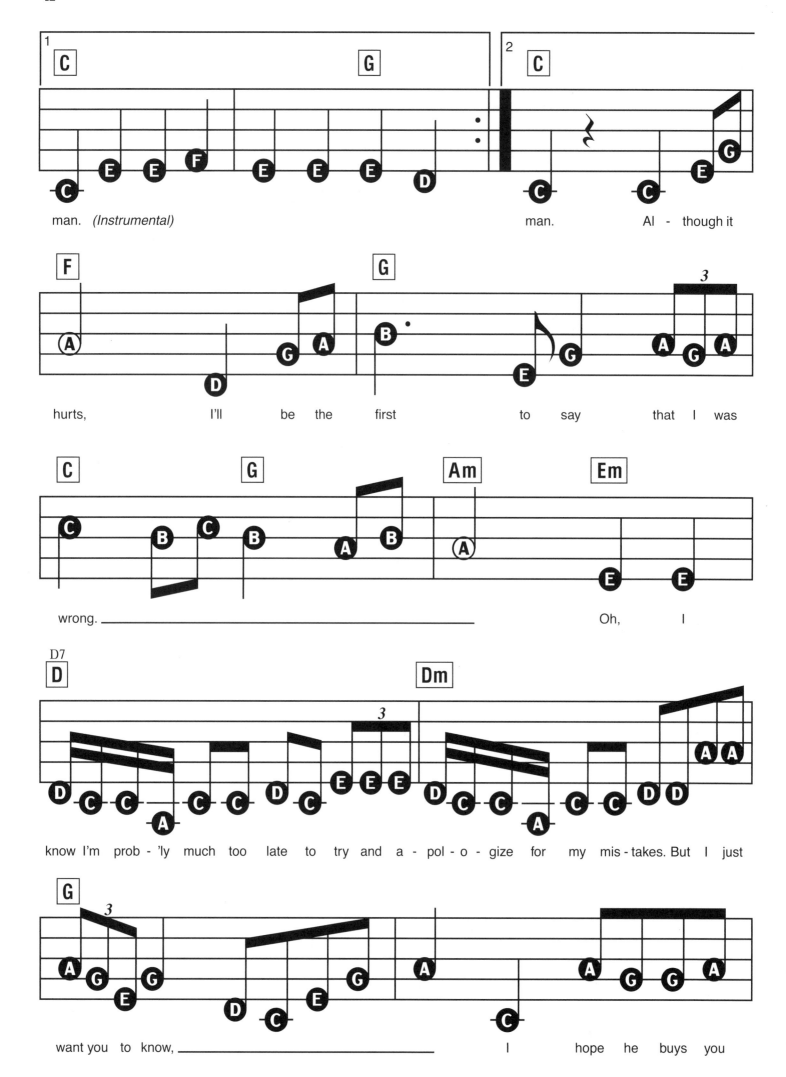

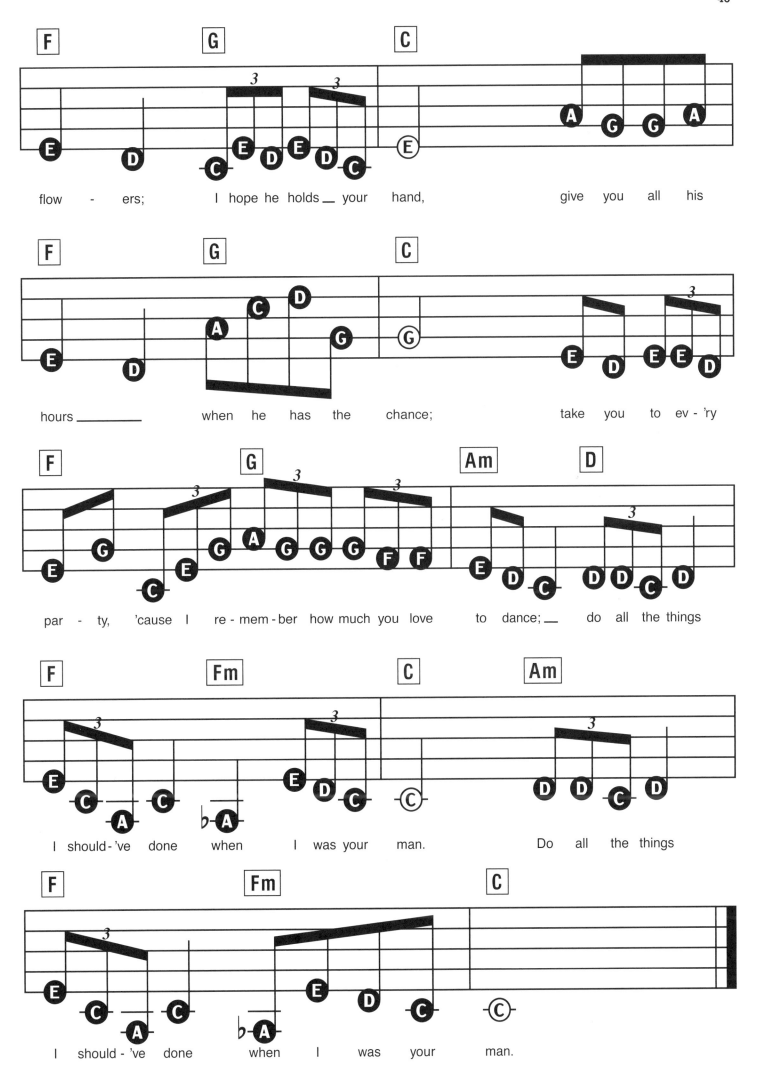

Marry You

Registration 8
Rhythm: Rock or Dance

Words and Music by Bruno Mars,
Ari Levine and Philip Lawrence

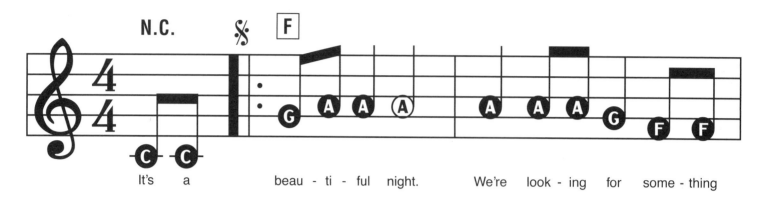

It's a beau - ti - ful night. We're look - ing for some - thing

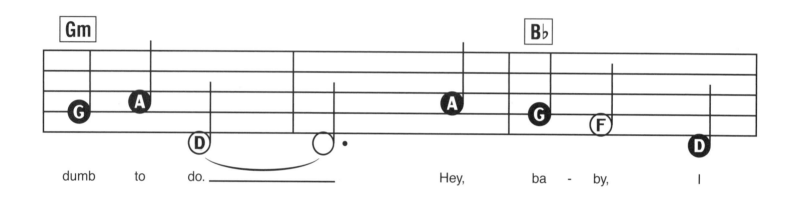

dumb to do. _____ Hey, ba - by, I

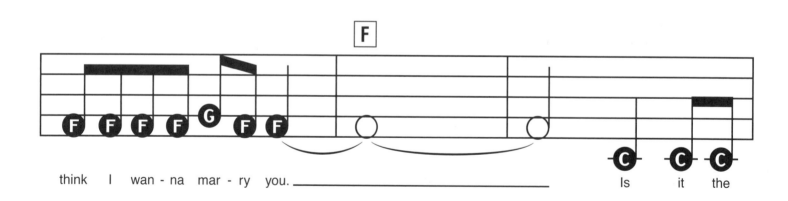

think I wan - na mar - ry you. _____ Is it the

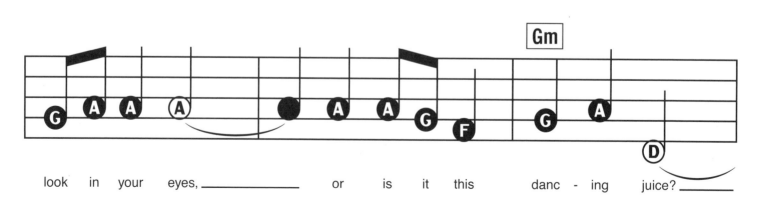

look in your eyes, _____ or is it this danc - ing juice? _____

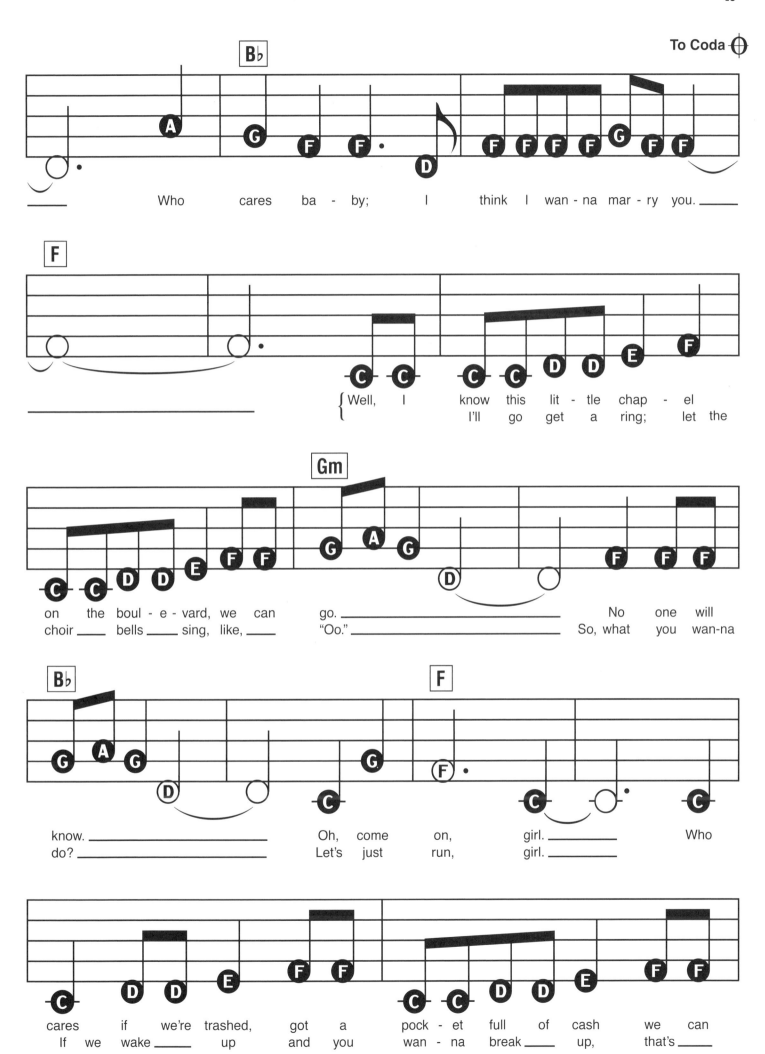

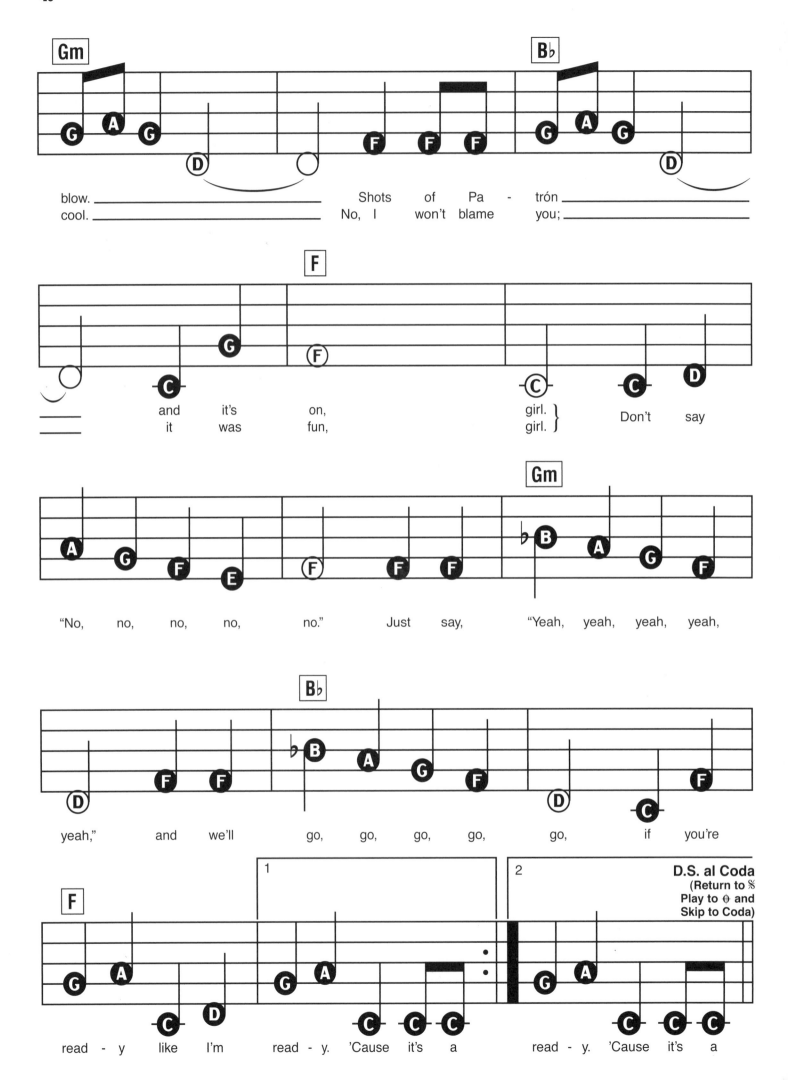

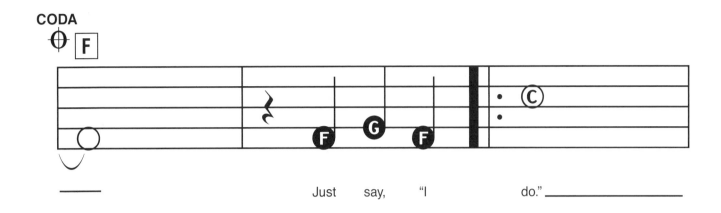

Just say, "I do." _____

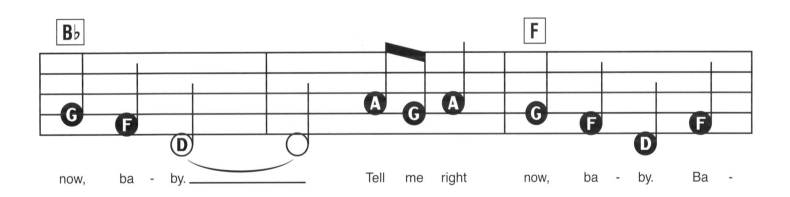

Tell me right

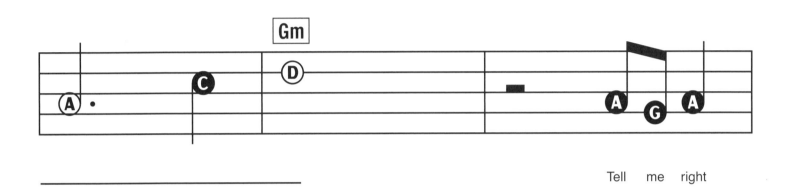

now, ba - by. _____ Tell me right now, ba - by. Ba -

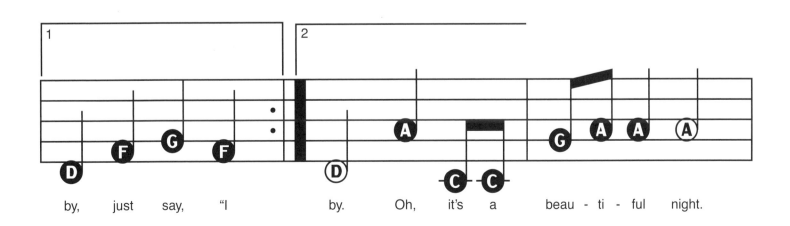

by, just say, "I   by. Oh, it's a beau - ti - ful night.

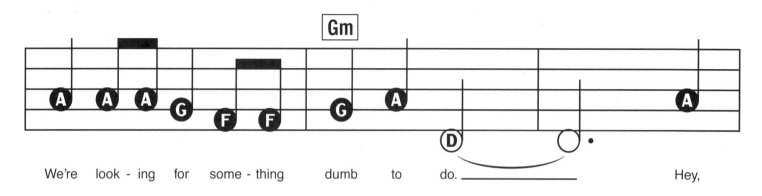

We're look-ing for some-thing dumb to do. _____ Hey,

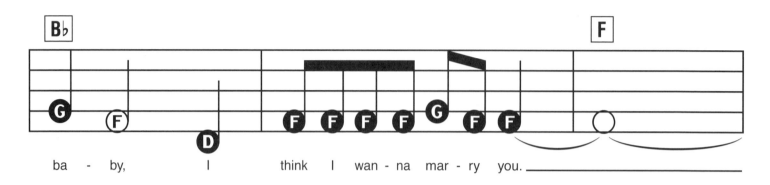

ba - by, I think I wan-na mar-ry you. _____

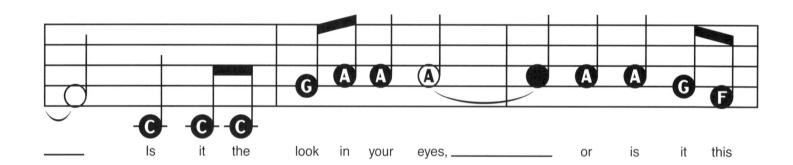

_____ Is it the look in your eyes, _____ or is it this

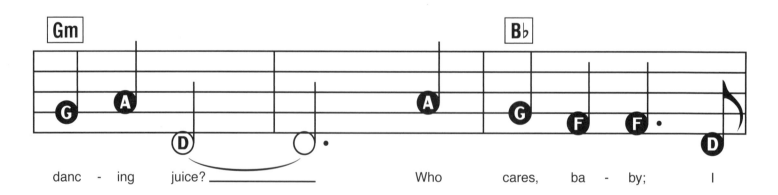

danc - ing juice? _____ Who cares, ba - by; I

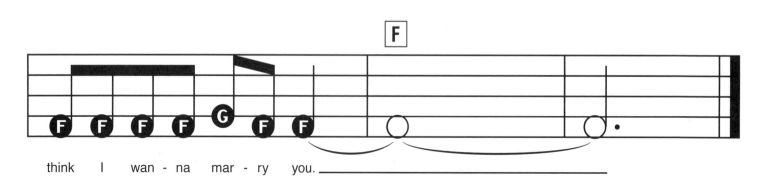

think I wan-na mar - ry you. _____